Solvang

Solvang

by

Amy Marie Orozco

Solvang (*Tourist Town Guides*®)
© 2011 by Amy Marie Orozco
Published by: Channel Lake, Inc., P.O. Box 1771, New York, NY 10156-1771
http://www.touristtown.com

Author: Amy Marie Orozco
Copyeditor: Kate St. Clair
Cover Design: Julianna Lee
Maps: Eureka Cartography
Page Layout Design: Mark Mullin
Publisher: Dirk Vanderwilt

Front Cover Photos:
"Wine Country" © Amy Marie Orozco
"Danish-Style Building" © Shutterstock/Dwight Smith
"Windmill" © iStockphoto.com/dbuffoon
Back Cover Photo:
"Items for Sale" © Amy Marie Orozco

Published in April 2011

ISBN-13: 978-1-935455-21-9

Disclaimer: The information in this book has been checked for accuracy. However, neither the publisher nor the author may be held liable for errors or omissions. *Use this book at your own risk.* To obtain the latest information, we recommend that you contact the vendors directly. If you do find an error, let us know at corrections@channellake.com

Channel Lake, Inc. is not affiliated with the vendors mentioned in this book, and the vendors have not authorized, approved or endorsed the information contained herein. This book contains the opinions of the author, and your experience may vary.

Help Our Environment!

Even when on vacation, your responsibility to protect the environment does not end. Here are some ways you can help our planet without spoiling your fun:

★ Ask your hotel staff not to clean your towels and bed linens each day. This reduces water waste and detergent pollution.

★ Turn off the lights, heater, and/or air conditioner when you leave your hotel room.

★ Use public transportation when available. Tourist trolleys are very popular, and they are usually cheaper and easier than a car.

★ Recycle everything you can, and properly dispose of rubbish in labeled receptacles.

Tourist towns consume a lot of energy. Have fun, but don't be wasteful. Please do your part to ensure that these attractions are around for future generations to visit and enjoy.

How to Use this Book

Tourist Town Guides® makes it easy to find exactly what you are looking for! Just flip to a chapter or section that interests you. The tabs on the margins will help you find your way quickly.

Attractions in this book may have an address, website (🖱), and/or telephone number (☎). If there is no contact information, please see the attraction or section heading.

Must-See Attractions: Headlining must-see attractions, or those that are otherwise iconic or defining, are designated with the ★ Must See! symbol. The author and/or editor made these and all other qualitative value judgments.

Coverage: This book is not all-inclusive. It is comprehensive, with many different options for entertainment, dining, shopping, and so on, but there are many establishments not listed here.

Prices: At the end of many attraction listings is a general pricing reference, indicated by dollar signs, relative to other attractions in the region. The scale is from $ (least expensive) to $$$ (most expensive). If the attraction is free, if no pricing information is available at the time of publication, then the dollar scale is omitted from the listing.

With the notable exceptions of gambling and wine tasting, most of the attractions in Solvang are family friendly. However, this does not guarantee meeting any kind of standard for you or your family. It is suggested to contact all establishments directly for further information if you have questions.

Acknowledgements

Huge thanks and appreciation go out to the many people who shared their love and knowledge of Solvang and its special surrounding areas with me. This book could not have happened without them. Not all names can be listed, and, no doubt, some that should be in print won't be—I apologize for that. In no particular order, these fine folks include Tracy Farhad of the Solvang Conference & Visitors Bureau; Nerissa Sugars from the Chumash Casino Resort and Spa; Linda Jackson, Solvang Chamber of Commerce; Brad Vidro, Solvang City Manager; Kathy Mullins, The Book Loft, Hans Christian Andersen Museum; food columnist Elaine Revelle; Jim Fiolek, Santa Barbara County Vintners' Association; architect Earl Petersen of Petersen Village; Laura Kath, Mariah Marketing; and all the other many shop owners, vintners, employees, wine pourers, food servers, residents, and visitors who shared their insights and opinions about the place they love.

From the keeping the home fires burning front, my husband, Alonzo, really went beyond the call of duty in all kinds of support and unconditional love. *Mil gracias* to my very generous cheerleading mom, Rickey Johnson, and all my siblings: Kaylyn, Greg, Doug, Chris, Mary (who was born on a windmill), and Jay (the golfer). Dad, I know you are looking down and smiling from that big winery in the sky. Loving friends, relatives, caring neighbors, and understanding clients really helped make writing this book the fun project it was. Thanks a million!

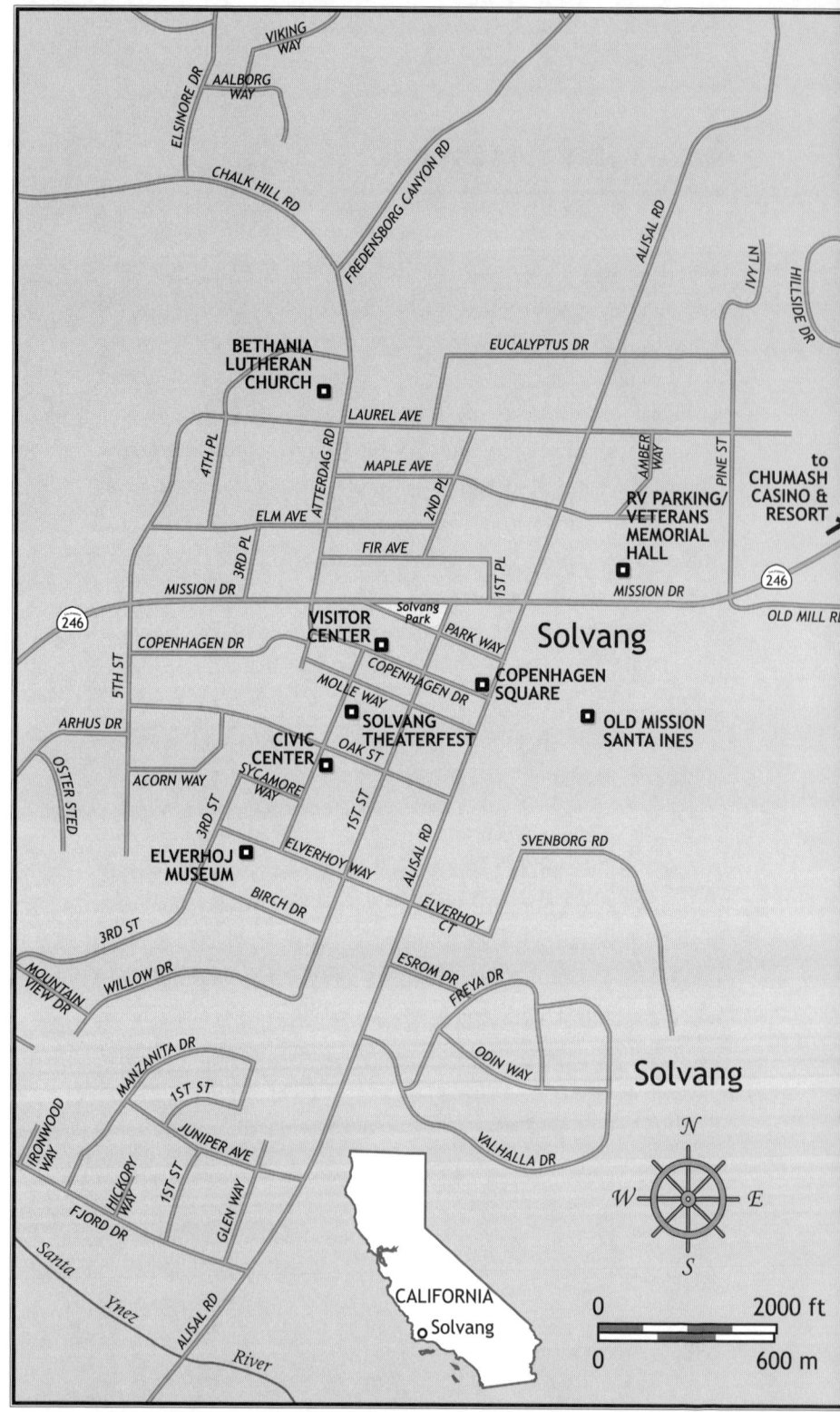

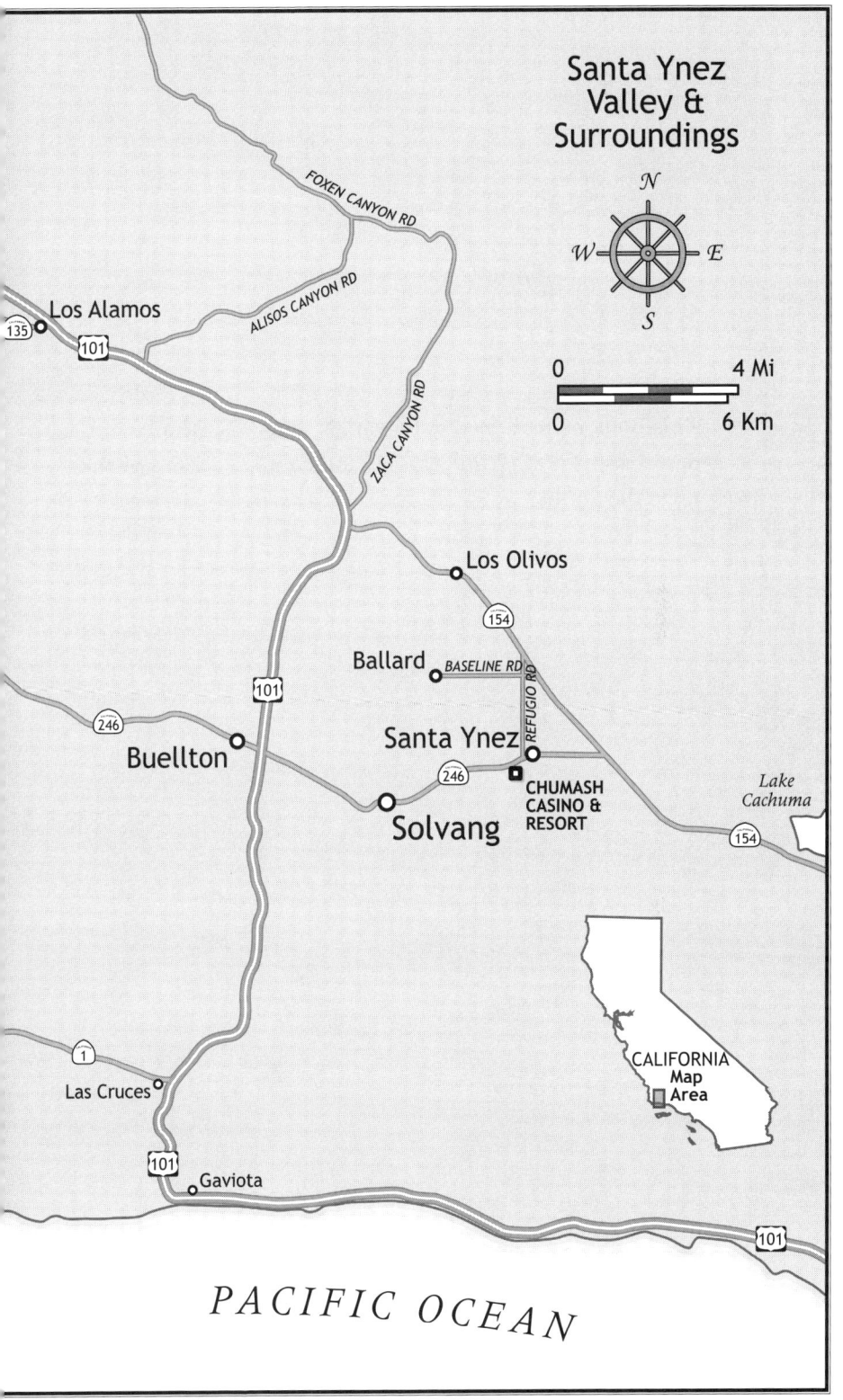

Santa Ynez
Valley &
Surroundings

N

W — *E*

S

0   4 Mi

0   6 Km

FOXEN CANYON RD

ALISOS CANYON RD

ZACA CANYON RD

135

Los Alamos

101

Los Olivos

154

Ballard   *BASELINE RD*

REFUGIO RD

101

246

Santa Ynez

Buellton

246

Solvang

CHUMASH
CASINO &
RESORT

*Lake
Cachuma*

154

CALIFORNIA
Map
Area

1

Las Cruces

101

Gaviota

101

PACIFIC OCEAN

This book is dedicated to Solvang's pioneers, whose wonderful spirit is very much alive and running strong in the town they built.

Table of Contents

Introduction

Velkommen a Solvang! Situated slightly inland along California's Central Coast in Santa Barbara County, Solvang is the Danish capital of America. This spotlessly clean town has been enchanting visitors for decades with its Old World charm living in the architecture, bright vivid flower gardens, friendly faces, and bustling bakeries. Founded in 1911 by a group of Danish educators looking to build a folk school, *solvang* means "sunny fields" in English. Sunny not only refers to the town's almost year-round perfect weather but also to the disposition of its residents.

Sometimes erroneously referred to as a Danish Disneyland, Solvang unintentionally earned a spot in the heart of the tourism industry. After the town's Danish Days celebration was featured in a 1947 *Saturday Evening Post* magazine article, readers wanting an anthropological peek of their own started to visit Solvang. From this authentic heritage, motels with windmills and lederhosen-like restaurant uniforms came forth. Today, the hamlet is a bit contrived but its Danish roots are strong and entrenched in the community. In fact, Danish royalty has visited three times. Also, bakeries continue to pump out sweet treats and the best bread, the Danish language is still heard in the Village, and visitors are always welcome.

"How welcome are visitors?" one may ask. For starters, they feel so welcome that well over 1 million of them come to Solvang every year. And it is not just because all the parking in Solvang is free and that there are plenty of public restrooms.

Since the turn of this century, the road down Danish memory lane as the reason to visit Solvang has been widened considerably. Today, the wine country also drives the tourism trade in the town with windmills. Little did those Danish educators know that those sunny fields would produce tons of grapes that would get made into world-class wine.

In 2004, the sleeper Hollywood hit *Sideways* catapulted Solvang and the rest of the Santa Ynez Valley into the wine-tasting destination stratosphere. The area eventually would have come into its own as the wines aged and the word spread through the grapevine. The movie sped up the process, however, and visitors reap the benefits. Unlike their Northern California counterparts, the Santa Barbara County vintner, vineyard owner, or a family member is on hand to pour a taste for a guest. Though days of free tastings are a thing of the past (which has a lot to do with crowd control), the nominal tasting fee in the Santa Ynez Valley is less than half of what's typically charged in Napa or Sonoma counties.

The beauty of Solvang extends beyond what the eye sees. Think Old World charm and manicured landscapes against the backdrop of rugged California mountains, rolling hills of coastal scrub, and vineyards. Beauty also lies in what one does not see. Notice the absence of chain stores, billboards, gas stations, and 7-Elevens, just to name a few.

Velkommen is a word taken seriously by Solvang. Residents are happy to share their inside knowledge of their town and are eager to voice their opinion on what they consider the best that Solvang has to offer. Get out there and talk to them.

History Lesson

The basic history for most of coastal California south of San Francisco can be divided into four parts: the First People, the Spaniards, El Rancho Days, and Modern Day. Specific to the Solvang story are the Danish immigrants who, in 1911, began settling in Solvang, situated in the Santa Ynez Valley. One hundred years later, the town's history continues to evolve and tell new tales, most recently that of becoming a premier wine tasting destination.

THE FIRST PEOPLE

It is believed that the first human settlers in North America arrived between 27,000 and 12,000 years ago. They came from Asia via a strip of land connected to Alaska, working their way down the Pacific Coast. The Chumash settled in the greater Santa Barbara area about 13,000 years ago. Their sophisticated and complex civilization emerged about 3,000 years ago.

Brightly colored rock paintings, most of which are estimated to be less than 1,000 years old, tell stories of the Chumash past. There are many Chumash rock and cave paintings in the area. Because they are a fragile cultural resource, rock art site locations are not revealed, with the exception of Painted Cave State Historic Park on the mountain between Solvang and Santa Barbara. (Directions to the site are at sbnature.org.) The cave is sealed with an iron gate but the rock art is clearly visible especially with a flashlight. Curators ask for no flash photography.

The Chumash population was exterminated to near extinction after the Spanish missionaries began their quest to spread Catholicism throughout California. As a result, most writings, legends, or stories that told the history of the Chumash people are incomplete.

The Chumash inhabited the area in California from Malibu in the south, Paso Robles to the north, the San Joaquin Valley to the east, and the Pacific Ocean to the west. They also lived on the Channel Islands. In an area of about 7,000 square miles, according to the history of the Santa Ynez Band of Chumash, the population numbered in the tens of thousands and they lived in about 150 scattered and independent villages. The villages spoke different but related languages.

Not surprisingly given the resources of the Pacific Ocean, the Chumash were excellent fisherman and boatbuilders. Their boats, called *tomols*, are canoe-shaped, and the Chumash used the natural tar seeps to seal the wood planks. These are the same tar seeps that dirty the feet of Santa Barbara beach goers today. Because their geographic location afforded them many natural resources, the Chumash had more time to develop crafts and other specialties such as tomols, beads, baskets, and tools, among other necessities of life.

From this culture of craftspeople grew a complex society. There was a social hierarchy with a chief, who could be a man or woman, on top of the pyramid and manual laborers on the bottom. The Chumash are also known for trading shells and creating a money system based on these seashells. This money system enabled trade to expand far beyond Chumash boundaries. The "cash" was minted from the purple olivella seashell. It is believed that the origin of the word *chumash* means "bead maker" or "seashell people."

The Chumash were also accomplished basketry artisans. Taking their engineering skills to a bigger task, they used whalebones to reinforce the roofs of homes made from willow branches. Like many people, the Chumash developed ceremonies to honor the seasons, such as fall harvest or a solstice.

The systematic decimation of the Chumash people and culture started in the 1770s, when Father Junipero Serra instituted the Catholic mission system in California. Missionization of the Chumash was between 1772 and 1822. During this period, the First People were forced into labor, who else would build the missions? Christianity was imposed, replacing Chumash spirituality and beliefs, and Spanish became their language. (The last known speaker of the Chumash language, Maria Ignacio, died in 1965. In the 1950s, the last full-blooded Chumash died.) Other aspects of European culture, such as food and dress, were forced on the Chumash as well.

The Santa Ynez Band of Chumash Indians reservation was established by executive order in 1901. They are a tribal government and an independent sovereign nation.

THE SPANIARDS

The first known written record of Europeans in California is from the diary of Juan Rodriguez Cabrillo, who sailed the coast of Southern California from 1542 to 1543. Cabrillo, from Portugal, sailed on behalf of the Kingdom of Spain. Between 1542 and 1769 there was occasional trade between the Chumash and passing Spanish ships up from Mexico, which was a Spanish colony at the time. While the Spaniards were busy plundering Central America and Peru for gold— still undiscovered in California—the Chumash were pretty much left alone for a roughly 200-year period.

Then, upon hearing that Russian ships had landed on the Pacific north coast of the United States in the mid- to late 1700s, Spain decided to protect "its" land. The Russians had an interest in the furs of the plentiful seals and otters found in the waters off California.

To keep California their own, part of the Spanish strategy was to convert the indigenous people—that is, the Chumash in the Solvang area—to their way of life. And, the California mission system was born. The construction of the first mission, in San Diego, was in 1769. Spain invaded California, then part of Mexico, and three years later the first white settlers came to live with the Chumash.

Missions were not built in geographical order. In the greater area around Solvang, Mission San Luis Obispo, north of Solvang, was constructed in 1772. Then, south of Solvang, Mission San Buenaventura was built in 1782 and Mission Santa Barbara in 1786. Mission La Purisma Concepcion, located west of Solvang, was built in 1787, and Mission Santa Inés in 1804. When the Mexican War of Independence ended in 1822, the Spanish period also ended in California.

EL RANCHO DAYS

Now a part of Mexico, the large land tracts (the missions) held by the Catholic Church were distributed by Pio Pico, the Mexican governor of California. These 500 land grants were given to various well-connected families as a thank you or a favor. These families' names, such as Alvarado, de la Guerra, and Carrillo, appear on street signs, parks, canyons, and towns all over California. The land grants became working ranches and mark the beginning of California's El Rancho days. Most of the ranches were cattle-raising operations.

The U.S.–Mexican War lasted less than a year and gave the United States control of California in 1848. The California gold rush started in 1848, and California gained statehood in 1850. The Santa Barbara region became known as a center of agriculture in the 1880s. As California's reputation for wonderful weather spread and burgeoning industries such as film and oil development provided employment, the Golden State's population grew. It was basically an agricultural state at the turn of the twentieth century.

THE STORY OF SOLVANG

As with other ethnic groups, Danish settlements were common in the United States during the large immigration of Western Europeans in the late 1800s to the early 1900s. Danish settlements, more than a means of survival, served to preserve Danish traditions and help new immigrants acclimate to life in the United States.

Solvang was founded as such a settlement in 1911 after Danish educators bought 9,000 acres of the Mexican land grant Rancho San Carlos de Jonata for $40 an acre. The educators planned to build a folk school, where the customs and language of their homeland would be preserved and passed down to future generations. Ninety-seven Danish-Americans laid down roots in Solvang within one year. They earned their livelihood while building the town of Solvang through carpentry, farming, milking, and baking.

Soon, the settlers quickly built a Lutheran Church and a folk school. The temporary folk school is now the site of the Bit O'Denmark restaurant on Alisal Road in the Village. In 1914, the temporary folk school gave way to Atterdag College, which, in addition to being a place to preserve Danish ways and to learn the ways of the new homeland, served as a boarding house, gymnasium, and social center for the community. As families grew and more immigrants arrived, the town developed and flourished. World War II interrupted Solvang life when many men left to serve in the military. Solvang's Danish look surfaced after World War II, when architect Ferdinand Sorensen returned from service in Europe and incorporated some of the Old World charm on buildings in the town.

TOURISM

The town's silver anniversary was the inaugural Danish Days Celebration in 1936. It is estimated that crowds of up to 40,000 descended on Solvang to celebrate the town's 25th birthday party. Danish Days is a weekend celebration of Solvang's history and Danish heritage. Danish Days continued its popularity and served as a stepping stone to Solvang's immense popularity as a tourist draw. In 1947, the *Saturday Evening Post* magazine ran a profile on Solvang highlighting, in glorious color, a Danish Days celebration. The artwork featured folk dancers. From that day forward, Solvang's status as America's Danish capital was established. Danish Days continues today and still attracts big crowds.

After the *Saturday Evening Post* story, tourists became a regular sight and their dollars a major part of the economy. Solvang's popularity as a car trip destination continued to blossom in the 1950s and 1960s. Happy to oblige this new stream of revenue, Solvang business owners expanded their operations. New restaurants and motels constructed with Danish themes were built to accommodate the visitors. The windmill at Copenhagen Square went up in 1963.

The energy crisis of the 1970s put a crimp on road trips, and the tourist dollars started falling off. Solvang answered this by upping the tourist ante and building more attractions and reasons for visitors to visit the town with windmills. Opened in 1974 and approached in a "build it and they will come" manner, the Solvang Festival Theater was one of such projects. Today, the theater is a vibrant venue in Solvang's list of visitor attractions.

The Danish blood pulsing through Solvang has thinned some-what, but its cultural ties to Denmark remain strong. Solvang and Aalborg, Denmark, enjoy a Sister City relationship. Local fraternal and social organizations have Danish ties. There are the Danish Brotherhood and Sisterhood Lodges, Dania Men's and Ladies' Lodges, and a Solvang chapter of the Rebild National Park Society. Rebild National Park is in Denmark.

TOURISM TURNED *SIDEWAYS*

Grapes and wine have been in the Santa Ynez Valley since the early days of Mission Santa Inés. In the 1970s and 1980s, however, more seeds of that cash crop were sown and the infrastructure of a specific wine region began construction. Harvest celebrations and crush parties came and went without much fanfare outside the perimeter of the valley, until the early part of the new millennium when *Sideways*, the sleeper hit of 2004, opened on the big screen.

In the film, two friends experience mid-life crisis during a wine-tasting trip through the Santa Ynez Valley—a final bachelor outing before one of them ties the knot. *Sideways* is directed by Alexander Payne and stars Paul Giamatti, Thomas Haden Church, Virginia Madsen, and Sandra Oh.

Turn Solvang sideways, and the rest of the Santa Ynez Valley, the film did! Seemingly overnight, the sleepy valley's roads were filled with vehicles navigating the wine trails. Still sleepy, the region retains its rural character and wineries remain family run operations.

Today Solvang enjoys its double appeal as the Danish Capital of America and a great wine country destination. There aren't many places in the world where the vineyards of world-class wines have views of windmills and the aromas from a cluster of Danish bakeries.

Area Orientation

⭐

The "Village" is what comes to most minds when speaking of Solvang. The four-square-block area is the heart of the Danish Capital of America and where the Danish pioneers first settled. The Village is the area bounded by Mission Drive/Highway 246 to the north, Elverhoy Way to the south, 5th Street to the west, and Alisal Road to the east. It is next to impossible to get lost in the neatly laid out streets. If feeling a little turned around, look for one of four windmills, a hanging basket of brightly colored flowers, or follow the aroma of freshly baked goods.

Solvang incorporated as a city on May 1, 1985. Located 46 miles northwest of Santa Barbara, it lies about 15 miles north of the Pacific Coast. (Santa Barbara has a south-facing beach, so sometimes the directions seem a little peculiar.) The city has an area of 2.5 square miles, and sits at an elevation of 505 feet. Solvang's population is roughly 5,335, with 52 percent females and 48 percent males. The median age of the residents is 43.8 years. Befitting a tourist town, retail trade accounts for 85 percent of the industry in Solvang.

WHEN TO VISIT

Any time is a good time to visit Solvang. As the "sunny fields" name indicates, on average there are 340 days of sunshine a year. Like the rest of California, however, when it rains, it pours. The wettest months are January, February, and March. Summer months, festival days, and weekends are busy times when the sound of tour buses is inescapable. The cooler months allow for more of a feel of old Denmark and the sidewalks aren't so crowded. Better deals on lodging can be found, too. Depending on interests, it may make more sense to visit Solvang at a specific time of year; for example, Danish Days and grape harvesting are part of the fun of fall, while December offers a wonderful Christmas celebration.

THE WEATHER REPORT

Though the mercury can rise into triple digits during the summer and can plunge below freezing in the winter, Solvang's weather is best described as mild. The sun shines more often than not, and rainfall is usually relegated to the first few months of the year. The town enjoys lots of sunshine throughout the year with clear, warm days and cool nights. Average temperatures vary between 54° and 76°F with highs reaching the upper 80s and winter lows in the 40s. Annual rainfall averages less than 12 inches. The highest recorded temperature was 115°F in 1971, and the lowest was 16°F in 1990. August is the warmest month and December is the coolest. February has the most rain at an average of about 5.5 inches. The driest month is July at .01 inch of rain.

No matter how high the mercury rises during the day, chances are it will be cool in the evening. At the minimum it will be sweater weather. The marine layer/fog creeps in over the night, and the damp chill can feel colder than the thermometer reads.

With the exception of June, summer months, including September, are typically tinderbox dry and wild fires can be a danger. February is the wettest month, though January, February, and March all have been known to bring flooding, with damage to crops and roads.

ANNUAL EVENTS

There is always something going on in Solvang, whether it is a time-honored occasion or an impromptu jam session in the park. Preparations for annual events typically begin the previous year. Great pride and attention to detail in planning are why events are so successful and enjoyed by so many.

MARCH: TASTE OF SOLVANG

**(Solvang Conference & Visitors Bureau ☎ 805.688.6144
📱 SolvangUSA.com)** Since 1982, on the third weekend of March there has been a celebration of Danish and local foods, wines, and live entertainment at the Taste of Solvang. The Friday night kickoff is typically a dessert reception with live entertainment. Big appetites are tested on Saturday with the Walking Smorgasbord, which is a series of taste stops around the Village. Following that is the Wine Tasting Room Walk on Saturday night. As somewhat of a recovery day, Sunday is a bring-your-own-picnic affair in Solvang Park.

APRIL: VINTNERS' FESTIVAL

**(Santa Barbara County Vintners' Association ☎ 805.688.0881
📱 sbcountywines.com)** Held the third Saturday in April, the Santa Barbara County Vintners Festival technically is not always a Solvang event. The location of the big white party tents can vary year to year, but they remain close enough for the celebration to spill into Solvang, leaving a big wine stain of fun. The idea behind the festival is to gather as many people as possible to taste as many of the local wines as possible. Wine education can be a lot of fun in Solvang.

MAY: RANCHEROS VISTADORES

(☎ 805.962.3000) Rancheros Vistadores is about observing not participating, unless you are member of the elite Rancheros Vistadores, a social club of rich, powerful men that includes former presidents and titans of industry. Based on the old rides of bringing cattle to market, Rancheros Vistadores began in 1930. Nowadays, typically in the first week of May, about 800 "cowboys" on horseback meet for a blessing at Old Mission Santa Inés and then head north for 20 miles or so to the group's private campground. The pageantry and parade make quite a show in the streets of Solvang.

AUGUST: OLD MISSION SANTA INÉS FIESTA

(1760 Mission Dr. ☎ 805.688.4815 🖱 missionfiesta.org) Mission Fiesta is a homegrown affair with activities geared toward children and families. As the church's largest fundraiser of the year, its proceeds are earmarked for restoration projects at historic Misson Santa Inés. The fiesta is a one-day affair and a tradition for many families.

SEPTEMBER: DANISH DAYS ✪ Must See!

(The Village ☎ 805.688.6144 🖱 solvangUSA.com) Danish Days is three days in the middle of the month devoted to honoring the motherland—her heritage, customs, and everything Danish. Intended to preserve Danish heritage, the annual event, begun in 1936, honors the establishment of Solvang by Danish-Americans in 1911. Thousands of visitors join locals in *aebleskiver* (a Danish-type of pancake ball) eating contests and aebleskiver breakfasts. An average of over 15,000 aebleskiver are served during Danish Days. Parades for each day of the celebration are held, including an adorable children's parade.

The legacy of Hans Christian Andersen is kept alive with storytelling hours that bring to life children's favorite fairy tales.. The historical reenactment group Ravens of Odin brings the time of the Vikings to life—and it wasn't a softer, gentler time. The Ravens can tell you the difference between chainmail and leather protective wear that the Vikings wore. Actually, depending on whom they were battling, the Vikings used both—and other—types of armor. Most of the festivities are in the Village, and typically sleepy Solvang parties loudly for the entire celebration. Old world artisans, traditional dancers, and musical performers inspired by Nordic sagas are part of the show too. There is a large Kids Korner tent with tables and tables of Lego toys. Games and refreshments are provided by local nonprofits. In addition to aebleskiver, there are booths, tables, tents, and picnic baskets laden with food of all nationalities. In the past, admission has been free to all events. At this time of year, the weather in Solvang is still very hot until the sun sets.

DECEMBER: SOLVANG JULEFEST
(Throughout the Village ☎ 805.688.6144 🖰 solvangUSA.com)
The Danes do up Christmas right. After all, isn't Santa Claus from that corner of the globe? In the spirit of saving the best for last, Julefest, also known as Winterfest, is a monthlong end of the year celebration. The theme is unabashedly Christmas. On the first Friday of December, a tree lighting ceremony, dance performances, and musical entertainment kick off the four-week party. The Julefest parade follows on Saturday. The town is lit up like, well, a Christmas tree—white fairy lights adorn trees, shops, restaurants, rooftops, and any and everything else outside. Outdoor carolers and musicians add to the

festivities, and retailers get into the spirit with open houses and special promotions. Santa Claus visits the Village, and other activities include a parade, a Nativity Pageant, and caroling.

GETTING TO SOLVANG

Though closer to Los Angeles, 132 miles, than to San Francisco, 297 miles, Solvang's just-off-Highway 101 location makes it a perfect getaway for residents of both metro areas. Automobile or tour bus is the most popular way to arrive. The town also is served by Amtrak Thruway Bus, and the Santa Barbara Airport is 40 miles away.

BY CAR

From the south (Los Angeles and Santa Barbara), visitors can take Highway 101 to Highway 154 in Santa Barbara over the San Marcos Pass, make a left on State Highway 246, and proceed approximately six miles to Solvang. Or, travelers can take Highway 101 up the coast to State Highway 246, turn right, and drive three miles to Solvang. Both routes offer beautiful scenery. Motorists can make a loop by taking one way into Solvang and returning home the other way.

From San Francisco, Santa Maria, and other northern points, head south on Highway 101. Take the Highway 246 off-ramp, which is about 26 miles south of Santa Maria. Go east (left) to Solvang.

BY AIR

Traveling to Solvang by air is expensive. The small **Santa Barbara Airport** *(500 Fowler Rd., Santa Barbara* ☎ *805.967.7111* 🖱 *flysba.com, Airport Code: SBA)*, about 40 miles east/south of Solvang and the even smaller **Santa Maria Airport** *(3217 Terminal Dr., Santa Maria* ☎ *805.922.1726* ☺ *santamariaairport.com, Airport Code: SMX)*, about 35 miles north of Solvang are the closest airports with commercial jet service. Private aircraft can land at **Santa Ynez Airport** *(900 Airport Rd., Santa Ynez* ☎ *805.688.8390* ☺ *santaynezairport.com, Airport Code: IZA)*, which is about three miles from Solvang.

United and Allegiant Air serve Santa Maria Airport. The airlines serving the Santa Barbara Airport are Alaska Airlines, United, US Airways, Frontier, and American Airlines.

Central Coast Shuttle *(*☎ *805.928.1977)* offers transport to Solvang from both airports. Numerous rental car and taxi companies serve the airports too. Don't count on any public transportation to or from either airport.

BY TRAIN

Amtrak *(*☎ *800.872.7245* ☺ *amtrak.com)* offers service via the Santa Barbara and San Luis Obispo train stations by connecting bus service to and from Solvang (SLV). Solvang's Amtrak bus stop is located in the heart of the Village at 1630 Mission Drive, also known as Highway 246. The Santa Barbara train station (SBA) is located at 209 State Street in Santa Barbara; the San Luis Obispo train station is located at 1011 Railroad Avenue.

BY BUS

Santa Barbara's Metropolitan Transit District (MTD) provides **The Valley Express** *(*☎ *805.963.3366* ☺ *sbmtd.gov)*, an early morning and late-afternoon bus for commuters to Santa

Barbara. There is no Greyhound Lines bus service to or from Solvang.

BY BIKE

Solvang is a popular destination for amateur, hobbyist, and professional cyclists. Swarms of uniformed cyclists silently and speedily sailing by are a common sight in the streets.

Bikes can follow the same route as a car or blaze their own new trail. For tips, tricks, itineraries, and information visit sbbike.org, santabarbaracarfree.org, and ridesb.com. See also "Pedaling Two Wheels of Fun" in the Outdoor Recreation chapter.

GETTING AROUND TOWN

Solvang's Village is compact and easy to walk; however, it is advisable to have a car to explore the surrounding area. Because the most convenient way to get to Solvang is by car, you are likely to have one during your visit. Parking throughout town is free, and even the off-the-beaten-path spots are not too far from the action. RVs are welcome to park for free in Solvang during the day at the Veterans Memorial Hall parking lot, 1745 Mission Drive, directly across from Mission Santa Inés.

SANTA YNEZ VALLEY TRANSIT

(☎ 805.688.5452 🖱 syvt.com) Santa Ynez Valley Transit provides limited service along Mission Drive in Solvang. The bus line connects Solvang to other towns of the Santa Ynez Valley, such as Lompoc, Buellton, Los Olivos, Ballard, and Santa Ynez.

CHUMASH CASINO SHUTTLE

(☎ 877.642.7748 ♥ chumashcasino.com) The casino offers a limited service shuttle. Schedule is subject to change, so please call in advance if you plan to use this service.

TAXI SERVICES

If wine tasting, consider hiring a taxi. In the Wine, Wineries, and Tasting chapter there are more suggestions about companies providing tours. Check the Outdoor Recreation chapter for information on renting bicycles.

Solvang Taxi (☎ *805.688.0069* ♥ *solvangtaxi.com)*, **Promenade Cab and Taxi** (☎ *805.616.0032* ♥ *promenadecab.com)*, and **Casino Cab** (☎ *866.747.8294)* offer taxi service in and around Solvang and the Santa Ynez Valley.

WHAT TO PACK

Like most of California, where comfort is prized over style, the dress code in Solvang is casual. Leave the cocktail attire at home. Walking shoes that can transition from sidewalks to bumpy, dusty winery roads are a must. Triple-digit summer temperatures dictate airy, loose cotton clothes. Winter weather calls for jackets and sweaters. The in-between rainy season from January through March necessitates shoes for bumpy, wet winery roads, along with umbrellas and proper outerwear.

No matter the season or what the daytime thermometer reads, in the evening it is a different story. The highest temperature will be "very cool" and can, and frequently does, dip into below-freezing range. Be sure to pack a sweater or jacket for nighttime.

When packing, keep in mind the following:

★ Sunscreen, sunglasses, and hats are a good defense against the typically bright sun shining over Solvang.

★ Swimsuits are required for the pool at the hotel.

★ Picnic basket, blanket, and corkscrew are perfect for a day of wine tasting.

★ Water bottle, helmet, and proper sports shoes fill the bill for bicycling or hiking.

★ Camera and binoculars are a must.

★ Necessary prescription medicines can't be easily refilled.

Don't worry, a forgotten item, incidental, or an unanticipated one most likely can be purchased in one of the many shops lining Solvang's streets.

FOR MORE INFORMATION

The **Solvang Conference & Visitors Bureau** provides valuable information on Solvang and the Santa Ynez Valley. Ask for the latest visitors guide (☎ *805.688.6144* ● *solvangUSA.com*). The Visitor Information Center is open daily from 9 a.m. to 5 p.m. From its location at 1639 Copenhagen Drive, a friendly face gives directions to restaurants, updates the latest activities, and points the way to the closest aebleskiver. The **Solvang Chamber of Commerce** promotes local businesses in the area (☎ *805.688.0701* ● *solvangcc.org*). Also check out the website for the **City of Solvang** (🖱 *cityofsolvang.com*). The **Santa Ynez Valley Visitors Association** has plenty of information, too. (☎ *805.686.0053* 🖱 *santaynezvalleyvisit.com*). For wine-specific information, contact the **Santa Barbara County Vintners' Association** (☎ *805.688.0881* 🖱 *sbcountywines.com*).

*The annual **Danish Days** festival is devoted to honoring the motherland—her heritage, customs, and everything Danish.*

It's a Danish Thing

The people of Solvang are proud of the town's Danish heritage and work hard to keep it alive. An extended invitation is always out to visitors to join in the cultural celebration, which can be found in Solvang's daily life, museums, and special festivals.

MUSEUMS

Solvang museums defy the stuffy stereotype. Built out of respect and made with love, they are interactive, intended for all, and public participation is encouraged. The museums are easily accessible and an integral tool in keeping the Solvang story alive.

ELVERHØJ MUSEUM OF HISTORY & ART ✪ Must See!

(1624 Elverhoy Way ☎ 805.686.1211 🌐 elverhoj.org) A couple of blocks off the Village's beaten path, stands the Elverhøj Museum of History & Art, whose mission is to feature the history and Danish culture of Solvang and to promote the arts. The Elverhøj (pronounced *el-ver-høy*) is the former home of Danish-American artists Viggo Brandt-Erichsen and his wife, Martha Mott "Patt" Brandt-Erichsen. Immaculately clean, colorful, and quaint are a few words that first come to mind when describing the Elverhøj. In the Solvang Room, the town's past is told in a variety of formats, including poster-size photos, video, artifacts, and models. The Early Room represents a Danish home, circa 1870s. The Diorama Cottage behind the main building has a model of 1920s Solvang. It is interesting to see the solid infrastructure built by the town's original architects and how it remains intact today. The museum's art exhibits are regularly rotated. Featured artists and their works are not confined to Danish inspiration, motif, or subject. A variety of classes at the museum do double duty promoting the arts and preserving Danish culture. Popular classes include lace making, floral design, beaded jewelry making, conversational Danish, and smørrebrød—Danish open-faced sandwiches. There are also art programs and other activities for children. The museum store offers a good selection of Scandinavian jewelry, linens, cookbooks, traditional Danish items, and Christmas goods. Open Wednesday through Sunday. $3 suggested donation.

HANS CHRISTIAN ANDERSEN MUSEUM ✪ Must See!
(1680 Mission Dr. ☎ 805.688.2052 ♻ bookloftsolvang.com)

Once upon a time there was a bookseller who lived in a land known as the Danish Capital of America. This bookseller so loved books and all things Danish he created a place of honor for the most famous storybook writer in the entire world— Hans Christian Andersen. That magical place, called the Hans Christian Andersen Museum, is where there are priceless treasures, including the famous man's original manuscripts and handwritten letters. So happy this bookstore owner made the people of the Danish Capital of America, that every year on April 2 they gather at this magical place to celebrate the birthday of Hans Christian Andersen. Cake is served to all.

Well, maybe it didn't happen quite like that, but the Hans Christian Andersen Museum is worthy of a chapter in a book penned by its namesake. Located on the town's main drag on the floor above **The Book Loft**, itself a hallowed neighborhood haunt, the museum promotes the work of the beloved writer of children's stories and books in addition to a better understanding of the man.

Highlights of the museum include many first and early editions, a variety of illustrated editions, and books in Danish. In addition to the bibliophilic items, there are a "Princess and the Pea" model, a representation of Hans Christian Andersen's home, a display of photographs of Andersen, and antique tools for making wooden shoes. There's also an exhibit on Andersen's (unrequited) love, Jenny Lind, the "Swedish Nightingale," who sadly never returned his affections.

Andersen's birthday, April 2, is a yearly celebration at the museum and the public is invited. Geared for the under-age-10 set, the birthday celebration includes a storyteller and birthday cake. Open daily. Donations appreciated.

CULTURALLY SPEAKING

Solvang's pioneers planted deep cultural roots that are still bearing fruit today. Authentic in origin, the fabric of Solvang and its way of daily life is Danish at its core. Experience the Danish side of life.

BETHANIA LUTHERAN CHURCH
(603 Atterdag Rd. ☎ 805.688.4637
⸙ hwy246.net/users/bethania/legacy.htm) Two blocks from the Village, the sundrenched white building of Bethania Lutheran Church is not only a place of worship for the townspeople; it is an excellent example of Danish architecture and a testament to the strong faith of Solvang's Danish forefathers. Sightseers are welcome to visit but Bethania is first and foremost a place of worship. The congregation was incorporated in 1911, and the church building was completed in 1928. Services were

held at the Atterdag Folk School, now the Solvang Lutheran Home, before the church was built. Fashioned after a church in Denmark, the church was built by local labor and craftsmen. As is common in many Scandinavian churches, a ship hangs from the ceiling, representing the prayers and gratitude of the seafaring people. It is said that such ships symbolize a haven of safety across the waters of life. Also of interest in the church are a pipe organ, whose numerous pipes stand around the perimeter of the choir loft, and beautiful stained-glass windows.

SOLVANG VILLAGE FOLK DANCERS

(☎ 805.688.7994 🖱 svfolkdance.com) Clad in late-1800s period Danish costumes, this dance troupe performs folk dances on Solvang streets and at special events. Sometimes called "the clog dancers," the group takes over Copenhagen Square on the third Saturday of the month (usually) from the middle to the late afternoon. The stage is not a formalized spot at all. Copenhagen Square is the roomy sidewalk area near the big windmill on Alisal Road where Copenhagen Drive dead-ends. The troupe unceremoniously appears (though the period costumes tend to make a statement and draw attention), musicians start to play or music is cued on a recording device, dancing commences, and people gather to watch. The dancers' joy is infectious and soon the sidewalk audience spills into the street. There's no set schedule, marquee, or any signage announcing the performance. The idea behind the Solvang Village Folk Dancers is to share their love of traditional dances. The public is welcome to participate, children are particularly encouraged. During short breaks, dancers happily pose for pictures with anyone who asks—no fee is charged.

The troupe also gathers for dancing on Saturday nights at **Veterans Memorial Hall.**

CHECK OUT THE ARCHITECTURE

A large part of Solvang's charm hinges on the visual appeal of the architecture and design in the Village, which is the downtown cluster of shops, restaurants, parks, lodging, and other businesses. So important is this aesthetic to Solvang's economic well-being, there are city-government design guidelines ensuring uniformity.

The design of the Village is based on Old World building styles found in Denmark and other Scandinavian countries. (Danish Modern is not a design option in Solvang.) Key elements to the specifics of exterior design include half-timbered logs, steep-pitched roofs, thatched roofs, copper-top roofs, dormer windows, and windows with beams in between panes of glass. Windows should be deep set to give the appearance of thick walls in addition to being divided into horizontal and vertical panes. Window boxes, hanging baskets, and other landscape containers are preferred for greenery and floral touches. The plants and flowers in them are to be vivid in color. Other preferred traditional garden elements include topiary, espaliered plants, sundials, birdbaths, and fountains.

Unlike the Northern European countries Solvang is trying to emulate, the area's climate has scorching hot summers and sunshine most of the year. This prompts the addition of canvas awnings over doors and windows. According to city code, "such awnings shall be of a solid color, sloping, open-ended variety with a straight valance."

It's a Danish Thing

It's a Danish Thing

Part of the Village's Old World charm is the pedestrian-friendly feel. Wide sidewalks encourage strolling and shopping. Crosswalks make it is easy to navigate the traffic, and curbs are wheelchair accessible. Many of Solvang's architectural delights are above pedestrian level, though. Roof design and décor tell other stories. For example, almost like weather vanes in their positioning, artificial storks, with and without nests, roost on the roofs and chimneys of commercial buildings and private residences. Storks play important characters in Danish folklore and are believed to bring good luck. Some of that good luck is in the form of bringing a baby to the house.

To keep the look of the Village special and unique, traditional Danish or Scandinavian design is discouraged in other parts of Solvang. Those areas are defined by Spanish mission and early-California ranch styles.

The flags lining Solvang's streets are hard to miss. A common decorative item, the flags of both the United States and Denmark are proudly displayed across Solvang. Fun fact: Denmark's flag, the 13th century Dannebrog, is the oldest state flag in the world still in use today.

THE BACKSTORY ON SOLVANG'S ARCHITECTURE

When Solvang's original Danish settlers began building their town in 1911, they did so in the manner of the styles surrounding them—Spanish mission, early-California ranch, or a close combination of the two. **Bethania Lutheran Church**, completed in 1928, was the first structure based on Danish architecture.

The quaint look of an Old World Danish village didn't pop up in Solvang until after World War II, and its debut was somewhat of a laughingstock. Why someone would build something so Old Country like that amused residents. A Nebraska native, architect Ferdinand Sorenson is credited with bringing Danish Provincial style to Solvang. Returning from Europe, he built his home in Danish style and constructed the first of the Village's four windmills. There is a plaque honoring the architect at **Ferdinand Sorensen Square**, located at 451 Second Street. An excellent example of his handcrafted woodwork is at **Solvang Restaurant**, 1672 Copenhagen Drive. Sorensen was knighted by the Queen of Denmark in recognition of his work.

Following Sorensen's lead, American-born local architect Earl Petersen put Danish facades on old buildings. Visitors to the town loved the look, which helped feed a new economic base of tourism. Earl Petersen is the architect of Petersen Village, in addition to other noted buildings in the Village. The foundation of Solvang's architectural integrity may be questionable, but the ensuing attention to detail and commitment to the real thing often surprises the Danish visitor, causing many to remark that "Solvang is more Danish than Denmark."

Solvang's status as a Preserve America community also vouches for its architectural authenticity. Preserve America is a federal initiative encouraging and supporting efforts to preserve and enjoy America's priceless cultural and natural heritage (preserveamerica.org).

A SUGGESTED WALKING TOUR

The best way to take in Solvang's special buildings and homage
to the architecture of Denmark is on foot. This suggested tour
is intended for a less than a half-day stroll. Indeed, it could
be knocked out in an hour if pressed for time. The timing
depends on the number of detours taken into stores, wine
tasting rooms, and restaurants along the way, not to mention
the length of time chitchatting with shopkeepers and other
friendly faces. The streets of Solvang are filled with all kinds
of retail temptations. There are plenty of public benches for
resting tired feet, too. If possible, start early in the morning.
It is fun to watch the shopkeepers prepare for a day of business—sweeping the sidewalk and setting out their merchandise,
plus bakery smells are at their peak earlier in the morning.

In addition to the homegrown Old World–style buildings,
spotless sidewalks, and attractive flowerpots filled with bright
blooms, some of the sights in Solvang are replicas of landmarks and architecture in Denmark. Don't keep your sights
strictly at street level, though. Much of the detail and charm of
the architecture is on the roof and in the roofline itself. Stork
statues on the roofs are good luck symbols.

Orient yourself at **Solvang Park**, located at Mission Drive
and First Street and close to plenty of free public parking.
There is a public restroom in the park, too. For a mini history
lesson on Solvang, visit the statuary and markers dotting the
park. The flagpole is dedicated to World War I survivors. Near
the gazebo, the Foundation Tablet celebrates the 25th year of
Solvang's founding. The bust of world-famous storyteller Hans
Christian Andersen serves as a popular gathering spot. Across
from the park on First Street is the Clock Tower with a brick

facade. The chiming clock tower and adjoining building is the home of Solvang Antiques.

Go back to Mission Drive, turn right (east) and walk to Alisal Road, where the stoplight is. Cross the street to the Little Mermaid statue in front of Denmarket Square. Solvang's Little Mermaid statue is a one-third-size replica of the original that sits on a rock in the Copenhagen harbor. Visitors to the statue in Denmark are surprised at just how small the Little Mermaid statue is, as are visitors in Solvang surprised at the diminutive sculpture.

Head south on Alisal Road, crossing back over Mission Drive. Alisal Road is one of Solvang's oldest streets. *Alisal* is a Chumash word meaning "grove of sycamores."

In the next couple of blocks on the opposite side of the street is a windmill. (The post office is just beyond that.) Behind the windmill is the **Round Tower** at 436 Alisal Road. This is a one-third-size replica (there's that dimension again!) of the famous *Rundetårn*, which translates as Round Tower. Located in Copenhagen, the Rundetårn was built as an astronomical observatory in the 17th century by Christian IV. The rebus, or word puzzle, on the Round Tower is explained in a plaque in the plaza, where Tower Pizza makes its home.

Walk west on Copenhagen Drive, taking in the Danish touches such as barn door entrances to shops, brightly colored store-fronts, and thatched roofs. At 1683 Copenhagen Drive, go through the little passageway to see a reproduction of Hans Christian Andersen's childhood home. On the south side of Copenhagen Drive, a few blocks down at Second Street is the big blue windmill known as Hamlet Square.

Continue west on Copenhagen Drive. Where the street curves at Atterdag Road is the beautiful glass-enclosed **Greenhouse Café**, which is part of Petersen Village. Petersen Village and its shops and hotel were built to resemble a Danish community. Meander through **Petersen Village Inn** courtyard with its half-timbered storefronts to Mission Drive.

To the west along Mission Drive are beloved examples of architecture designed to invite cars off the highway to a place of business. The **Viking Motel,** with its rooftop Viking ship, is an excellent example of this. Fans of this style use the term Roadside Vernacular Architecture, others use the term kitschy.

Across Mission Drive from Petersen Village is another iconic Solvang windmill. This is the home of the new Solvang Brewing Company. A few more steps eastward and you are back where you started—Solvang Park on the opposite side of the street.

Wine, Wineries, and Tasting

The secret to the success of the Santa Barbara County wine country is its Transverse Mountain ranges, which run east-west. As a result of its orientation, the Santa Ynez Valley grape-growing region has more sunlight but cooler temperatures, thanks to the ocean breeze that travels up.

Long before the movie *Sideways* cast Solvang into wine tasting fame, winemakers were practicing their craft and sharing the fruits of their labors with the public. Wine tasting was akin to being in someone's home and breaking bread with them. In fact, wine tasting used to be free (even in Napa and Sonoma counties). The inspiration was that it was educational. By helping to develop the consumers' palates and expand their knowledge, their appreciation of wine would expand and help cultivate the then-infant industry. Perhaps the guest would like the wine well enough to purchase a bottle, maybe a case, or more. From those humble beginnings came the feelings of intimacy and shared camaraderie while wine tasting. Until the movie *Sideways* hit the screen, anyway.

Laughing and talking while wine tasting are fine acceptable behaviors. Being overly drunk is not. Wine tasting should be entertaining, not the entertainment. Bachelorette parties, corporate reward events, and other raucous groups are common in tasting rooms across the wine country. Their numbers, though, don't make their manners acceptable. The wineries are taking back control. Unofficial rules such as "no bridal veils allowed" are being instituted and approaching limousines may trigger a quickly posted "Closed for private party" sign.

Outside of a private home or event, wine tasting takes place at a winery, tasting room, or wine bar. A winery is where the grapes are grown and turned into wine. Usually the tasting area is small with a bar and a few chairs, and most tasters are standing. Most likely there will be other items, such wine paraphernalia, to purchase in addition to wine. Generally speaking, a winery tasting room is located off-site and represents the wines of a single winery. A wine bar offers wines from a variety of wineries and may offer other alcoholic drinks. With the focus on wine, food is often an afterthought and may be limited to unsalted crackers. Conversely there could be a full menu available. Live entertainment is often featured on weekends. Indeed, some of the larger wineries are known for their full-scale outdoor concerts.

Whatever time of year you visit Solvang, most likely there will be a special event at a nearby winery. Harvest is typically celebrated the second Saturday in October, and the **Santa Barbara County Vintners' Festival** is typically the third Saturday in April.

A tasting usually includes about five to seven different wines, called a flight. The cost ranges from $10 to $20, which includes the glass at some wineries. It is perfectly acceptable to split a tasting between two people. Ask at your hotel for winery recommendations. In addition to giving insight, the person at the front desk also may have some special coupons or deals to share.

A FEW WINE WORDS AND THEIR DEFINITIONS

The more one wine tastes, the larger the oenophile nomenclature becomes. The following barebones vocabulary list will get the novice conversant in beginning wine tasting. After a few tastings, the words will roll off the tongue. Then they'll slur from the lips. The list assumes the reader knows the meaning of aroma, aftertaste, and similar cross-referenced words.

Appellation: A legally defined grape growing area. There are five appellations in Santa Barbara County. They are Santa Maria Valley, Santa Ynez Valley, Los Alamos Valley, Santa Rita Hills, and Happy Canyon of Santa Barbara.

Balance: The harmony of the wine's components: acid, sugar, tannin, alcohol, and flavor.

Body: The size or heft of the wine in the mouth. While a light-bodied wine glides over the palate softly and without weight, a full-bodied wine feels heavy and big in the mouth.

Bouquet: The smell or aroma of wine. Also called the nose.

Breathing: When the wine mixes with air to release flavors and aromas. Wine breathes easier when poured into a glass or decanter.

Legs: After swirling a glass of wine, rivulets or tears of the wine run slowly down on the inside of the glass. Those rivulets or tears are called legs. Legs indicate a rich wine.

Oenophile: A lover of wine.

Varietal: A wine made primarily from a single-named grape variety. Chardonnay and merlot are examples of a varietal.

TIPS ON TASTING

Wine tasting is fun. There's no reason to feel intimidated, particularly by pretentious snobs. If it makes a newbie feel better, remember that the people pouring the wine, sometimes the owner of the vineyard, would much rather be introducing their wine to a fresh palate than be stuck listening to a wine snob inebriated with their own verbosity.

Here are some basic steps to wine tasting. Before reading any further, make sure a designated driver is secured for the outing.

First, hold up the glass of wine and swirl it. This releases the wine's aroma, or bouquet. Notice the difference between picking up the glass and smelling it, and picking up the glass, swirling it, and *then* smelling it. Take note of how the "legs" run down the side of the glass.

Second, stick your nose into the glass and take a gigantic sniff. Digest the aroma. Take another big sniff. Differentiating between wines is more about smell than taste. Use your sniffer.

Next, take a sip. Slowly. Let the wine roll over all over your taste buds. Note the different tastes: sweet, peppery, jammy, floral… Massage the wine with your tongue.

Lastly, either spit or swallow the wine. Both are perfectly acceptable. It is also OK to have a small sip and pour the rest into the silver champagne-style bucket on the bar. (Some say spittoon is the official name for that, while others call it the pour bucket—sort of like the difference between sweat and perspire.)

GREAT GRAPES MAKE GREAT VARIETALS

Santa Barbara County doesn't specialize in one type of wine or grape. In the Santa Ynez Valley alone over 60 varieties of wine are produced. Popular wines include chardonnay, syrah, sauvignon blanc, cabernet sauvignon, cabernet franc, merlot, Riesling, pinot grigio, pinot noir, and viognier.

Cabernet franc: A major red grape. Usually it is blended with cabernet sauvignon and merlot to create a Bordeaux style. Tastes and aromas are peppery, raspberry, cassis, and tobacco.

Cabernet sauvignon: A thick-skinned grape from hardy vines resistant to rot as well as frost. Cabernet sauvignon is the offspring of cabernet franc and sauvignon blanc. It shares characteristics with both grapes, such as the black currant and grassy aromas.

Chardonnay: A green-skinned grape neutral in flavor. Its subtle tastes are associated with oak, apples, and pear, and can be described as buttery. Chardonnay is one of the most popular grapes in the world, and is an important part of Champagne and other bubbly wine.

Merlot: A red wine grape. It is used for blending and for varietals. Merlot aromas include berry, plum, and currant. In Bordeaux wines, merlot is a main grape. Merlot is one of the most popular varietals around the world.

Pinot grigio: A white wine grape also called pinot gris. Pinot grigio is refreshing and crisp with tastes of pear, peach, and apricot.

Pinot noir: A red wine grape. It is associated with Burgundy, France. A medium body wine with aromas of black cherry, berries, and currant.

Riesling: A white grape variety from the German Rhine region. Riesling is one of the world's top three white wines in the world. Chardonnay and sauvignon blanc are the other two. Riesling's aromas are described as apple, lemon, flora,

Wine and Tasting

and fruity. In addition to dry and sweet wines, it is used to make sparkling wines.

Syrah: A dark-skinned grape that makes powerful red wines. Syrah is popular around the globe. Aromas and tastes are peppery, blackberry, and cinnamon. Sometimes referred to as Shiraz.

Sauvignon blanc: A green-skinned grape. Its origin is Bordeaux, France. Sauvignon Blanc's taste is described as crisp and dry, or grassy, citrusy, and sweetly tropical. It was one of the first wines bottled with a screw cap.

Viognier: A white wine grape. Its strong aroma is floral, peach, apricots, and orange blossoms. California's Central Coast, which includes Santa Barbara County, is a leading producer of this grape.

TOURS

A wine tour can be an easy do-it-yourself affair. Pick up one of the many free maps available at the visitors center and hotels, and blaze a trail. Make sure there's a designated driver! Or, put yourself in the trusted hands of a tour guide. There are many different types of tours: night tours, backcountry tours, organic-only tours, and lots more. When shopping around for a tour be sure to ask about what is covered in the price—tasting fees, picnic lunch, is the price per hour or outing, which wineries will be visited, and will other parties be part of the tour. Reservations are typically required for tours.

Some tour companies specializing in the Santa Ynez Valley are **A Day of Wine and Horses** (☎ *805.688.5984* ● *wineand-*

horsetours.com), **Cloud Climbers Jeep Tours** (☎ *805.646.3200* 🖱 *ccjeeps.com)*, **The Grapeline Wine Country Shuttle** (☎ *951.693.5755* 🖱 *gogrape.com)*, **Santa Ynez Valley Wine Tours** (☎ *805.284.1270* 🖱 *enjoytheridesyv.com)*, **Stagecoach Co. Wine Tours** (☎ *805.686.8347* 🖱 *WineToursSantaYnez.com)*, and **Sustainable Vine Wine Tours** (☎ *805.698.3911* 🖱 *sustainablevine.com)*. Ask at your hotel for a recommendation or at a tasting room where the server was particularly helpful.

WINERIES

Without a "sour grape" in the bunch, all Santa Ynez Valley wineries are worth a visit. There are too many wonderful winery options in the Santa Ynez Valley, however, for the scope of this book. The following alphabetical listing is based on geographic proximity to Solvang. No matter which wineries are chosen to be explored, something will be poured to please the palate and the setting will be beautiful. Take a bet on the weather and plan to do it *alfresco*. Reservations are not necessary, though it is advised to call ahead for big groups of ten or more. Typically, wineries are open daily and their hours are 11 a.m. to 5 p.m.

BUTTONWOOD FARM WINERY & VINEYARD
(1500 Alamo Pintado Rd. ☎ 805.688.3032 🖱 buttonwoodwinery.com) More than a vineyard, Buttonwood is a working farm with pomegranates, peaches, livestock, and more. The rustic tasting room has a down-home feel. In the back is a huge garden and picnic area with—what else?—Buttonwood trees. Sauvignon blanc is the signature wine here. Green, sustainable, eco-friendly, biodynamic...Buttonwood

has been farming in that manner before any of those terms became buzzwords.

LINCOURT VINEYARDS

(1711 Alamo Pintado Rd. ☎ 805.688.8554 🖰 lincourtwines.com)
The big yellow house atop the little hill serves as the tasting room at Lincourt Vineyards. This is a quiet, pretty spot. The focus is on pinot noir and chardonnay, though other types aren't ignored. Inside the old farmhouse are two serving stations. Take your tasting outside to the surrounding lawn and garden, along with a packed picnic basket. The large veranda offers a nice view, too.

RIDEAU VINEYARD

(1562 Alamo Pintado Rd. ☎ 805.688.0717

🖰 **rideauvineyard.com)** An old-fashioned horse carriage is the marker pointing out Rideau Vineyard— and it's across the road from the Quicksilver miniature horse ranch. The vineyard is dedicated to Rhône varietals and is farmed sustainably. The tasting room is in a 200-plus-year-old adobe house. In one of the door's cutaways, the thick adobe is displayed. Founded by New Orleans native Iris Rideau, the tasting room has Crescent City decorating accents and more than a hint of Mardi Gras sensibility. A tapas plates menu is available.

RUSACK VINEYARDS ✪ Must See!

(1819 Ballard Canyon Rd. ☎ 805.688.1278 🖰 rusack.com) The long and winding road that leads to Rusack's door is worth the drive. This is one of the most beautiful settings in wine tasting. Outside the tasting room is a redwood deck with tables and chairs shaded by ancient oaks. Visitors are welcome to bring a picnic lunch and enjoy the pastoral view of the hills and vineyards while sipping the Syrahs, Sangiovese, sauvignon blanc, and other wines. Rusack also blends cabernet franc, merlot, and petit verdot into their own Bordeaux-style red, named Anacapa. Cheese and crackers are available for purchase inside the large tasting room. There are gift and wine-related items for sale, too. Rusack is a family-owned winery.

SHOESTRING
(800 East Highway 246 ☎ 800.693.8612

🖱 shoestringwinery.com) Shoestring is the first winery when approaching Solvang from the west. The tasting hours are limited—from 10 a.m. to 4 p.m. on Friday, Saturday, and Sunday. Some of Shoestring's wines include pinot grigio, rosé, cabernet sauvignon, Sangiovese, merlot, and Syrah. As with other wineries, picnics are encouraged at Shoestring. Sit under the olive trees.

TASTING ROOMS AND WINE BARS

There's nothing quite like a day spent visiting wineries, unless of course, there is not designated driver. If that's the case, it is best to stay on foot and visit the Village's tasting rooms and wine bars—there are plenty of them.

The Village has the perfect wine tasting trail, and not just because no car is necessary. It is a short walk between tasting rooms, sometimes just a matter of crossing the street or rolling next door. Small snacks or light fare may be available for purchase; count on water crackers being available to soak up some of the alcohol. Typically, tasting rooms are vineyard-designated and wine bars carry a number of different vineyards' wines. The following establishments are listed alphabetically. Unless noted otherwise, most establishments open daily at 10 or 11 a.m. and close by 5 or 5:30 p.m. Weekends can be crazy in a "good way," if boisterous crowds are preferred over the relative intimacy of a weekday.

CARIVINTAS WINERY TASTING ROOM

(476 First St. ☎ 805.693.4331 ☗ carivintas.com) The atmosphere at Carivintas is almost the direct opposite from what is expected in a tasting room. First, children and dogs are warmly welcome. Games, coloring books, and other distractions are available for the kids. Second, no pretentiousness is allowed. Offenders may be laughed out. Also, Carivintas stays open later than other tasting rooms in the Village. A part of its profits is donated to a variety of animal rescue nonprofits, and the label art features animals and wildlife scenes. Not to mention the loud and large animal art that decorates the space. Oh yeah, the wine… There is a nearby pinot noir–only vineyard. Other wines are made from grapes throughout California. Open daily until 7 p.m., later on Thursday through Saturday.

D'ALFONSO – CURRAN WINES

(1557 Mission Dr. ☎ 805.688.3494 ☗ D-CWines.com) This has some of the best people-watching windows in Solvang. They look onto busy Mission Drive and the nonstop trail of visitors on the sidewalk. The interior is large and the design is modern. There are two round bars for tasting. Some of the varietals offered are grenache blanc, pinot noir, pinot grigio, Sangiovese, Syrah, and tempranillo.

DASCOMB CELLARS

(1659 Copenhagen Dr., #C, entrance on First St. ☎ 805.691.9175 🖱 dascombcellars.com) Here's a comfy-cozy tasting room that's open later than most. This family-operated business owns one of the oldest cabernet vineyards in Santa Barbara County. Customers tasting at the end of the working day have the best chance to talk wine with vintner Dave Dascomb when he comes in from the fields. Closed Tuesday and Wednesday. Open until 7 p.m., sometimes later on weekends.

LIONS PEAK VINEYARDS WINE TASTING

(1659 Copenhagen Dr. ☎ 805.693.5466 🖱 lionspeakwine. com) The tasting room is in the heart of downtown Solvang but the vineyard (and another tasting room) is north in San Luis Obispo County. Lions Peak features Bordeaux varietals, Rhônes, Italian, port, and dessert wines. There is a large selection of wine-related accessories and gifts. Extended hours on the weekend.

LUCAS & LEWELLEN VINEYARDS ✪ Must See!

(1645 Copenhagen Dr. ☎ 888.777.6663 🖱 LLwine.com) Tasters can choose a list featuring reds, whites, or reserves wines; there are "fun" and "traditional" lists, too. While the over-21 crowd is sipping at the long bar, their offspring can hang out at the kids' table and do their own thing. Louis, the Lucas part of Lucas & Lewellen, is often behind the bar pouring wine and getting to know the guests—after he has finished in the field. There is a large retail space with high-end foodstuffs, kitchen and dining accessories, and wine paraphernalia. Extended hours on the weekend.

MANDOLINA

(1665 Copenhagen Dr. ☎ 805.686.5506 ⬤ mandolinawines.com)
Mandolina is Lucas & Lewellen's Italian sister and she lives just
a block away. The focus at Mandolina is estate-grown Italian
varietals. Some of these are barbera, dolcetto, nebbiolo, pinot
grigio, rosato, and toccata. Like her relatives, Mandolina's
tasting menu has different options for wine types. Not surprisingly, there are many Italian gift items for sale as well as
paintings, specialty foods, and wine-related items in the tasting
room. Open daily, later on the weekends.

OLIVE HOUSE

(1661 Mission Dr. ☎ 805.686.5159 ⬤ Olivehouse.com) Known
for its large selection of dessert wines, the Olive House has a
good selection of imported and domestic wines. The tasting
area is small. The surrounding selection of olives, olive and
other oils, vinegars, and other gourmet foods is impressive and
large.

PRESIDIO WINERY

(1603 Copenhagen Dr. #1 ☎ 805.693.8585 ⬤ presidiowinery.com)
The atmosphere at Presidio, with its stand-up bar, is friendly.
There are also plenty of tables and chairs in the spacious
tasting room. Here the lost art of conversation is kept alive.
This winery prides itself on certified organic and biodynamic
wines. Pinot noir, Syrah, and chardonnay are its specialties—
filtered and unfiltered. There is a retail selection of gourmet
treats, apparel, wine-related gifts and accessories.

ROYAL OAKS WINERY TASTING ROOM

(1651 Copenhagen Dr. ☎ 805.693.1740 🖰 royaloakswinery.com)
Despite its noble name, Royal Oaks is committed to making
the wine experience enjoyable for all. Situated next to the
Visitors Center, the tasting room has a good selection of retail
items. The dessert wine tasting is very popular at Royal Oaks.

SEVTAP

(1576 Copenhagen Dr., #1 ☎ 805.693.9200
🖰 **sevtapwinery.com)** This new tasting room specializes in
handcrafted wines in Bordeaux varieties. Sevtap's winery is in
Buellton, and the all the grapes are from the California Central
Coast. The tasting room has a fun atmosphere; for example,
blackboard-painted walls encourage chalk graffiti. It's an
inviting, lounge-ish kind of spot and gives a new twist to the
tasting room scene. Open Thursday through Monday from 10
a.m. to 6 p.m. Barrel tastings by appointment.

SORT THIS OUT CELLARS

(1636 Copenhagen Dr. ☎ 805.688.1717
🖰 **sorthisoutcellars.com)** There is a 1960s *Playboy* magazine feel
to Sort This Out Cellars, and it is not just the pinup art on the
wine labels. Nor is it the *Bachelor Pad* magazines neatly fanned
on the cocktail table in the High Rollers Lounge—that is, the
back room. It is the celebration of the time, albeit from a
rose-colored glasses point of view, when "men had character
and women had curves. A time when you could smoke, drink,
curse, and have a good time without apology," according to
their website. The blackjack games and casino nights keep with
this theme. There is no Sort This Out Cellars vineyard. They
buy their grapes and their most popular wines are cabernet

sauvignon, chardonnay, and merlot. Guests are invited to reserve the **High Rollers Lounge** and bring their own food to accompany a tasting. There are cheese trays for sale. Live music on weekends. Open daily until 7 p.m., 10 p.m. on Friday and Saturday.

TASTES OF THE VALLEYS WINE BAR

(1672 Mission Dr. ☎ 805.688.7111 ☗ tastesofthevalleys.com) The few steps down to below street level and the brick floor give this a true wine cellar feel. The fireplace makes it cozy. High-end wines from over 30 different wineries are available, as are cheese plates and other light snacks. Try a flight or a glass. Remember that they are pouring while many have stopped. Open daily until 8 p.m. on weekdays, later on weekends.

WANDERING DOG WINE BAR

(1539 Mission Dr., #C ☎ 805.686.9126

☗ **wanderingdogwinebar.com)** The overstuffed couches and board games encourage a leisurely wine tasting. The 40-plus wines by the glass and the over-200 by-the-bottle wines from around the world invite trying something new. The wines are described as "palate picked," which means each one has been taste-tested by the owners before being offered to visitors. Outsider ratings, scores, recommendations, and trends don't have anything to do with what's being poured. Themed tastings and blind tastings show learning can be fun. There's a light-fare menu, and an excellent selection of beers to boot. Open daily, and stays open late on weekends.

WEDDINGS AND OTHER SPECIAL EVENTS

It is hard to beat the romance of the wine country as a perfect setting to get married. Saying "I do" with a full moon rising over the vineyards is one picture-perfect option, and there are hundreds of other equally beautiful choices for that special day. Special events in the wine country are not just about weddings. This bucolic region is well suited to social events such as family reunions, reunions, *quinceañeras*, graduation parties, and special anniversaries. The business world isn't left out either. Who wouldn't raise their productivity to attend a conference, win a sales incentive prize, or be chosen for an executive retreat.

There are facilities to host events for up to 700 people. The venues include wineries, private estates, hotels, intimate inns, and parks, among others. In addition to the wineries listed in this chapter, two popular event sites are **Firestone Winery** (☎ *805.688.3940* 🖱 *firestonewine.com)* and **Sunstone Winery** (☎ *805.688.9463).* **Solvang Festival Theater** (☎ *805.688.4813* 🖱 *solvangtheaterfest.org)* and **Solvang Veterans Memorial Hall** (☎ *805.688.7529* 🖱 *cityofsolvang.com)* have the capacity for big crowds.

A full roster of professional event coordinators and wedding consultants are ready to be of service. Two of them are **Santa Barbara Wine Country Weddings and Events** (☎ *805.688.2934* 🖱 *sbwinecountryevents.com)* and **Classic Party Rentals** (☎ *805.688.7213* 🖱 *santabarbara.classicpartyrentals.com).* **Santa Ynez Valley Weddings** (🖱 *weddings.syv-online.com)* is an online source for local vendors and suppliers. For corporate events, **Relevé Unlimited** specializes in incentives and special event production (☎ *805.688.1434* 🖱 *releveunlimited.com).*

Solvang hosted the 2007, 2008, and 2009 Time Trial Stage of the Amgen Tour of California, the nation's largest professional cycling race.

Outdoor Recreation

That there would be plenty of outdoor recreation in a place whose name translates as "sunny fields" in English seems like a safe bet. There's a lot more activity going on in Solvang than wine tasting, eating, and shopping. Not only is the weather usually favorable but the scenery is gorgeous, too. Don't worry about finding room to pack recreational equipment, rentals are available in the Santa Ynez Valley.

PEDALING TWO WHEELS OF FUN

Solvang is a bicycling paradise. That's why superstar Lance Armstrong is a familiar face in town, as are the thousands of others who come to train and race. Solvang as a premier cycling destination and training ground is partially due to the availability of snow-free steep climbs in the surrounding Santa Ynez Mountains. The town hosted the 2007, 2008, and 2009 Time Trial Stage of the Amgen Tour of California, the nation's largest professional cycling race. It is slated to hold the 2011 time trials, too. The Tour of California brings in the caliber of cyclists who race in world-class events, including the Tour de France. Additionally, throughout the year there are major amateur races that cyclists use to condition for other competitions. Some cyclists have noted that the town's resemblance to a European village helps in the mental training for a race such as the Tour de France.

On the other side of the kickstand, Solvang is also perfect for the novice or hobby bicyclist. The Dan Henry Bike Route offers a leisurely ride from Solvang to Los Olivos. Pick up the route on Alamo Pintado at Mission Drive/Highway 246. (Dan Henry created the directional pavement markings used to guide bicyclists. He is considered a legend in bicycling circles.)

The Village's flat streets, pedestrian friendly thoroughfares, and easy-to-reach destinations make bike riding enjoyable. Enjoyable for the cyclists, that is. The long lines of fast-pedaling bike clubs and the slow, clueless four-wheeler Fred Flintstone-like-car drivers can be an annoyance to automobile drivers. Be sure to take care, and drivers, remember to Share the Road.

DR. J'S BICYCLE SHOP

(1693 Mission Dr. ☎ 805.688.6263 ● drjbikeshop.com) The signed Lance Armstrong jersey on the wall is an indication of how seriously this shop takes bicycling. However, the friendly, knowledgeable staff, which includes the owner, is very helpful. The full-service shop has bikes for sale and lightning-quick repairs to get cyclists back on the road. Their guided bicycle tours (including wine tours) and rentals arm of the business is down the road in nearby Santa Ynez *(☎ 888.557.8687 ● winecountrycycling.com).*

WHEEL FUN RENTALS

(475 First St. ☎ 805.688.0091 ● wheelfunrentals.com) This is the place to rent a surrey with the fringe on top. Different-sized surreys are available—a single bench seat for loving couples to three bench seats for the whole crowd. For the more rugged minded looking to blaze their own wine trail, mountain and road bikes are at the ready for rent. Other wheeled vehicles for hire are strollers, wagons, and wheelchairs. Open seven days a week from 9 a.m. to sunset. Hourly, half-day, and full-day rates.

SOLVANG GETAWAY BICYCLE TOURS

(☎ 805.245.7311 🖱 solvanggetawaybicycletours.com) Solvang Getaway Bicycle Tours can put together a weekend—or a week—of bike riding with all the necessary details, such as food and lodging, taken care of. There is a menu of preplanned tours. There are romantic tours, half-day tours, and the option to plan a custom tour. It is a beautiful, flat area to explore on a bicycle.

RIDING HIGH IN THE SKY

Need to clear your head and get a different perspective on things? How about a glider ride? Soaring silently above the beautiful Santa Ynez Valley with vineyards, windmills, Lake Cachuma, and the Santa Barbara coastline, it is easy to understand the meaning of the word bucolic.

WINDHAVEN GLIDER RIDES

(900 Airport Rd., Santa Ynez ☎ 805.688.2517 🖱 Gliderrides.com) Different flight lengths and itineraries are available. There's the 15-minute Scenic Flight that gives an overview of the area. The 22-minute Mountain Adventure climbs to 4,000 feet above the floor of the Santa Ynez Valley. Bring your camera. There are not many photo opportunities like this around. Limited hours year-round.

SWINGING A CLUB

Golf is played year-round in Solvang and the Santa Ynez Valley. So if there's room, pack the clubs! The setting for the four courses can't be beat and there are so many wineries to serve as the 19th hole. All the following courses have a pro shop, driving range, and offer lessons. Only Zaca Creek has no dining. As to be expected, green fees are higher on weekends. Weekend or weekday, reserving a tee time is highly recommended.

LA PURISIMA GOLF COURSE

(3455 Hwy 246, Lompoc ☎ 805.735.8395 🖱 lapurismagolf.com) Noted architect Robert Muir Graves designed this 72 par, 18-hole championship course. La Purisima is very tough. The course has hosted the PGA Q School, where golfers try out for the tour, a number of times. The wind comes up in the afternoon, so consider teeing off as early as possible. ($$)

RANCHO SAN MARCOS GOLF COURSE

(4600 Hwy 154, Santa Ynez Valley ☎ 805.683.6334 🖱 rsm1804.com) Famous designer Robert Trent Jones Jr. created the original blueprint for this popular 71 par, 18-hole course. From the greens, there is a beautiful view of Lake Cachuma and surrounding mountains. Watch out for the wildlife, deer, and wild turkeys, crossing the fairways. The occasional bald eagle is also spotted soaring overhead. Rancho San Marcos has a great practice facility with a super driving range, chipping green, and putting green. Here's a tip: Bearsback, hole number 15, is a beast of a hole. Green fees include cart and range balls. ($$$)

RIVER COURSE AT THE ALISAL

(150 Alisal Rd. ☎ 805.688.6042 🖱 rivercourse.com) Located in Solvang proper, the 72 par, 18-hole River Course is relatively flat but offers a good challenge. The course has four lakes and is situated along the softly winding Santa Ynez River, which is dry a good part of the year. Oak and sycamore trees offer shade on the course. Oh, by the way, the golfing scenes in the movie Sideways were filmed at River Course. ($$)

ZACA CREEK GOLF COURSE

(233 Shadow Mountain Dr., Buellton ☎ 805.688.2575 🖱 zacacreekgolf.com) A popular course with beginners and old duffers alike, Zaca Creek is an executive-style, 29 par, 9-hole course. The fairways are tree lined and there are no water hazards. For the benefit of youth golf, some holes are closed to play on certain afternoons of the week. Call to check on this. ($)

SKATING ON THICK CONCRETE

Sidewalks filled with shopping tourists are not the ideal place to skate[board]. A specially constructed course in a city park filled with trees is an ideal place to skate. Read the rules, and follow them.

HANS CHRISTIAN ANDERSEN PARK ✪ Must See!

(633 Chalk Hill Rd. ☎ 805.688.5575 🖱 cityofsolvang.com) The skate park part of this 50-plus-acre park is of special interest. That is, *skate* as in skateboarding. Helmets, kneepads, and elbow pads must be worn while skating. Also, skating must be confined to the skate park. No skating on curbs, parking lots, and entrances. Conversely, no bicycles are allowed in the skate park.

The park is located about a half-mile outside of the Village a little past where Atterdag Avenue turns into Chalk Hill Road as it travels north. A fairy tale gate serves as its entrance and a winding road dips down into the park. The gate is closed when it rains. One of the playgrounds has a variety of slides and interactive toys. A creek winds through the park. There is a group picnic area. Stately oak and sycamore trees dot the landscape. There is a grassy area, picnic tables, and grills scattered around the play area.

The massive park has two playgrounds, four standard tennis courts, an equestrian trail, horseshoe pits, picnic areas, and restrooms.

BACKDOOR BOARDSHOP

(1511 Mission Dr. ☎ 805.686.5886 🖱 bdboardshop.com) Decks, wheels, and apparel for skateboarding are for sale here. There is an equally good selection of surf and snow hard goods. The store advocates for these sports in the community.

PLAYING IN PARKS

Of course a family-centric community like Solvang has plenty of public parks. The intentionally low-tech parks are designed for romping, running, roughhousing, and recreating. They are well maintained, well used, safe, and don't cost a dime.

NOJOQUI FALLS PARK

(Alisal Rd., south of town ☎ 805.934.6211
🖱 Countyofsb.org/parks) Head out of town and past the Alisal Guest Ranch & Resort for some dusty fun. From the picnic tables of Nojoqui Falls Park it is about a 15-minute walk to the waterfalls. The flow of the falls coincides with the rain.

Typically this means a cascading rush of water in the late winter and spring with a brilliantly green park, and a slow-to-nary-a-trickle fall with a brown park in the summer and autumn. Even so, the waterfall is pretty all year round. The time when water isn't flowing strongly is when more mountain lions are spotted. They have to come closer to civilization to find water. So be on guard and heed the warning signs. The park is a great place for bird watching. Birders can expect to see blue jays, blue grosbeaks, owls, yellow-billed magpies, titmice, and woodpeckers. Along with the hiking trails and picnic tables at Nojoqui, there are ball fields, barbeque grills, benches, a playground, a group picnic area, and restrooms. Nojoqui Falls Park is open daily from 8 a.m. to sunset.

SOLVANG PARK
(Mission Dr. at First St. ☎ 805.688.5575 ♨ cityofsolvang.com)
This 1.14-acres of green is the heartbeat of the town. It is the center of action for community events such as **Danish Days** in September, **Julefest** (Winterfest) in December, and Free Friday Night Movies in the summer. During daylight hours there are always hand-holding couples strolling and mothers with strollers picnicking. The monuments and statues scattered around the park tell part of Solvang's story as a new town. There's a bandstand, a small play area, and restrooms, too. The City Christmas Tree is erected in Solvang Park.

SUNNY FIELDS PARK
(900 Alamo Pintado Rd. ☎ 805.688.5575 ♨ cityofsolvang.com)
Set the kids free at this 6.2-acres wide-open space constructed to fuel young imaginations. In a fenced off, kids kingdom area, Sunny Fields Park has a wooden castle, gingerbread house,

Outdoor Recreation

puppet theater, Viking ships, rock-climbing walls, monkey bars, and a variety of swings. The kids will have to dream up anything else they would need. The adjoining wide-open green space has a softball diamond and backstop. Check out the horseshoe pit and walking trails, too. In hot weather months, a sprinkler sprays water to cool things down. Pack a lunch and make use of the covered picnic tables with barbecues. There is a separate area with a large Santa Maria–style barbecue available, too. With all that fun going on, the pint-size clock tower is necessary to help keep track of the flying time. Sunny Fields Park is located outside of the Village.

Ententainment

Though asking about the nightlife and entertainment possibilities in Solvang is usually answered first with a chuckle and then "the town is closed by eight"—fear not! Entertainment does exist. One just needs to know where to look for the options such as concerts, live music, theater stage productions, and gaming. Actually, given its population, there are a lot of entertainment possibilities in the Santa Ynez Valley. So why does Solvang close at 5:30 p.m., anyway? Because that's the Danish way: work hard all day and afterward go home to family.

CHUMASH CASINO RESORT ✪ Must See!

(3400 E. Hwy 246, Santa Ynez ☎ 800.248.6274 ☷ ChumashCasino.com) Get the high standards of Las Vegas gambling without all the other stuff bogging you down. Bordering Solvang is the Chumash Reservation, home to the Chumash Casino Resort, which opened in 2004. This is where the big kids come to play. The casino is a 24-hour Las Vegas–style gaming heaven. A favored gambling destination, devotees come from far and wide to try their chance on winning large amounts of cash, a luxury car, or any of the regularly advertised high-priced prizes. Valet parking is free, and there are shuttles regularly making the short trip to and from Solvang.

PLACE YOUR BETS

Slots, table games, poker, and bingo are the siren calls of this 24-hours-a-day adult playground. Sorry folks, no dice games allowed. Players must be 18 and older to gamble. No alcohol is served or allowed in gaming areas. In an un-California twist, smoking is allowed on the second floor of the casino. The nonsmoking area is on the third floor. For more bang out of the betting buck, check out Club Chumash, a promotion offering discounts at retail outlets in the resort, gaming credits, and entry to car drawings and other prizes. It is free to join and comes with a membership card.

There are 2,000 slot machines in the casino on the second and third floors. New games make frequent debuts and to really up the ante, there is a High Limit Room with slot machines, too. There are over 100 slot machines in the no-smoking section on the third floor. As it is in most casinos, if not all nowadays, coins aren't used in the slot machines, so there isn't the sound of a rushing waterfall of coins when one wins the jackpot. Table games include the ever-popular blackjack, Ultimate Texas Hold'em, and Three Card Poker, among others. Played standard casino style, blackjack also has tables in the **High Limit Room**. Poker games are varied and plentiful at the casino's 14 poker tables. There are daily tournaments and the stakes vary all day, all the time. Popular games include 5-Card, Omaha High/Low, and Hold'em. Bingo is big at the casino. It is so big, in fact, the smoke-free bingo parlor, also known as the **Samala Showroom**, has seating for 1,000 players. Bingo games vary in theme and prizes; monthly schedules are available. Bingo is played Sunday through Wednesday. From Thursday to Sunday, the venue is used for stage shows.

APPEARING LIVE ON STAGE

The **Samala Showroom** hosts A-list headlining musical and comedy acts throughout the year. The 1,400-seat venue provides an intimate feel while still being big enough to bring the stars who sell out shows. Ticket prices vary by show and frequently sell out *fast*. Don't wait around to purchase tickets. Otherwise you'll miss the likes of Jay Leno, Diana Ross, Fleetwood Mac, and Tony Bennett. Championship boxing matches also bring in the sellout crowds.

AAAHH, THE SPA

The Spa at Chumash Casino Resort is the perfect respite from an overdose of wine tasting or gambling, but who needs a special reason to make a retreat. The 5,000-square foot, full-service spa offers massage, body treatments, skin care, waxing, manicures, and pedicures. Special spa packages are available and often offer a discount.

In addition to the pampering full body and reflexology treatments found at The Spa, the Samala Stone Massage is a signature Chumash spa treatment. It incorporates the Chumash Indian tradition of using warm stones and sage for healthy benefits. The Desert Sage massage oil is made from local plants.

The capsule wash is also of special interest. After a body treatment, when the body has absorbed as much of the essential oil it possibly can, there may be some left on the skin. To wash it off, one enters a kind of washing machine for humans, though the head sticks out and the body position is horizontal.

The entire menu of body scrubs, soaks, and facials is tempting. There are treatments customized for men, too. The upscale spa boutique has a wide selection of lotions, potions, gifts, books, CDs, clothing, and more.

It is not necessary to be a guest of the Chumash Casino Resort hotel to use the spa, though being at least age 18 is required.

Day passes are available for the fitness center, pool, steam room, and locker room. The spa is housed in the hotel building of the Chumash Casino Resort. Appointments are recommended (☎ *805.691.1755*).

LIVE MUSIC AND PERFORMING ARTS

That a town the size of Solvang has a professional theatre company, and such a good one too, is impressive. The variety of live theater productions includes musical, drama, comedy, and others.

Wineries and restaurants are popular venues for live music acts. Though not quite the scale of the headlining acts at the **Chumash Casino Resort**, some wineries host concerts whose main stars' name recognition reaches past the Santa Barbara County line. Smaller-scale performances at tasting rooms and similar venues are often advertised by flyers posted around town and small ads in the local papers. Ask around for any tips in the live music scene.

GAINEY WINERY
(3950 E. Hwy 246, Santa Ynez ☎ 805.688.0558
⏻ gaineyvineyard.com) Past concerts at Gainey have included the varied likes of Count Basie, Emmylou Harris, and Al Jarreau. Usually held in the warmer summer and fall months, the concerts are popular sellouts.

MAVERICK SALOON AND DANCE HALL
(3687 Sagunto St., Santa Ynez ☎ 805.686.1109
⏻ mavericksaloon.org) Country hospitality and Wild West fun

Windmill in Solvang *(© Amy Marie Orozco)*

Good Luck Stork on a Roof *(© Amy Marie Orozco)*

Solvang Clock Tower (© *Amy Marie Orozco*)

Wine Barrels *(© Amy Marie Orozco)*

Hans Christian Andersen *(© Amy Marie Orozco)*

Big Red Clog (© *Amy Marie Orozco*)

Solvang Trolley (© *Amy Marie Orozco*)

Vineyard (© *Amy Marie Orozco*)

Hamlet Square (© *Amy Marie Orozco*)

Bakery Window *(© Amy Marie Orozco)*

Dancing in the Street *(© Amy Marie Orozco)*

Solvang Architecture *(© Shutterstock/ artconcept)*

Solvang Winery *(© Shutterstock/ Julia Fikse)*

Solvang Building Ornamentation (© Shutterstock/Dwight Smith)

play at the Maverick every night of the week. For a real rootin' tootin' time, check it out on Saturday nights and don't forget to wear your dancing boots. The crowd at this cowboy bar is a different animal than the one wine tasting earlier in the day. Short on décor, big on atmosphere, the Maverick is large and loud with plenty of room for dancing and raisin' all kinds of fun.

PCPA THEATERFEST

(420 2nd St. ☎ 805.686.1789 ⬤ solvangtheaterfest.org) Pacific Conservatory of the Performing Arts (PCPA) Theaterfest runs June through September in the 700-seat, open-air theater located in the Village. The repertory group—with both professional actors and advanced students—stages drama, comedy, and musical performances. Theaterfest occasionally goes by several differnt names around town. The actual name of the theater is **Solvang Festival Theater**. The name of the nonprofit that runs the theater is Solvang Theaterfest. When PCPA performs in Solvang, they use the moniker PCPA Theaterfest *(⬤ pcpa.org)*. Just say "Theaterfest" and people will understand. In addition to the professional productions of Santa Maria–based PCPA, the sycamore-shaded Solvang Festival Theater is used for a variety of community events such as fundraisers, concerts, and theater workshops. Curtain is at 8 p.m. Limited engagements. Call or check website for performance schedules and tickets.

Bordering Solvang is the Chumash Reservation, home to the **Chumash Casino Resort,** *which opened in 2004.*

Solvang for Families

Solvang is no sin city, that's for sure. If anything, it is the opposite. Life in Solvang centers on family and activities for children. Healthy and wholesome amusements are what Solvang is about.

LET'S PLAY FARM

Small, family-owned farms, other than vineyards, make up a good deal of the land around Solvang. Some of these agricultural operations invite visitors to learn about the land and to experience the life of a farmer.

APPLE LANE FARM

(1200 Alamo Pintado Rd. ☎ 805.686.5858

🖱 **applelanesolvang.com)** The family that picks together stays together. The picking at this family-run farm begins in mid-August, though there's no predicting Mother Nature, and runs through October. Types of apples include gala in August, golden and red delicious in September running into October, and Fuji and Granny Smith in October and November. ($)

SOLVANG FARMERS MARKET

(Copenhagen Dr. and First St. ☎ 805.962.5354

🖱 **sbfarmersmarket.org)** Every Wednesday afternoon, the Santa Barbara Certified Farmers Market Association sets up on part of First Street in the Village. The market promotes family farms and gives the community the opportunity to shop and socialize. Produce doesn't get any fresher than this. There are also heirloom agricultural products and little-known vegetables. Free samples can help decide which one to buy. Open rain or shine. Hours are 2:30 to 6:30 p.m. in summer and 2:30 to 6 p.m. in winter.

MORRELL NUT & BERRY FARM

(1980 Alamo Pintado Rd. ☎ 805.688.8969) More farm picking fun at Morrell's. The season starts in June with raspberries and blackberries. In October and November walnuts are ready to be picked. If you don't want to pick your own, Morrell sells their goods at the **Solvang Farmers Market** on Wednesdays. ($)

HORSES BIG AND SMALL

Using the word *equestrian* might be a tad highfalutin' for these horse activities. Still, the kids can get up close and personal with their new four-legged friends. Maybe pet a mane, and definitely get their picture taken.

QUICKSILVER RANCH ✪ Must See!

(1555 Alamo Pintado Rd. ☎ 805.646.4002

☗ qsminis.com) Quicksilver Ranch is an excellent example of sharing the love—the love of miniature horses, that is. The owners welcome the public to view the miniatures and to wander around the 20-acre working ranch, which is dedicated to show and breeding stock. Miniature horses are affectionate, gentle—even with very young children, and make excellent pets. Don't call these equines ponies—a miniature's height must not exceed 34 inches from the base of mane to the floor. Foals are born between March and June. Guided group tours are available but must be scheduled in advance. Drive right into the ranch and find a place to park. Open seven days a week from 10 a.m. to 3 pm.

THE HONEN

(1639 Copenhagen ☎ 805.794.8958 🖱 solvangtrolley.com) The clip-clop sound heard around the Village is the Honen. *Honen* is the Danish word for a streetcar trolley drawn by two large Belgian draft horses. In Solvang, the just-under-30-minute ride includes a tour guide telling the story of Solvang. Information on routes and schedules, which can vary by season, can be found at the Visitors Center. Call about tours in French, Japanese, and Spanish. Sometimes the weather is too hot for the horses and the tours are suspended until the mercury drops. The Honen is also available for special bookings, such as weddings and rides through vineyards. From $9, there are discounts for seniors and children.

MUSEUMS CAN BE FUN

Nothing beats learning about history than being able to see the tangible items of the past. Museums really bring the subject matter alive. Plus, at these museums, kids don't have to worry about using their inside voices.

SANTA INÉS MISSION ✪ Must See!

(1760 Mission Dr. ☎ 805.688.4815 🖱 missionsantaines.org) Juxtaposed against the Village's bright, shiny, and scrubbed storefronts is the rustic, earth-toned Mission Santa Inés. The mission is number 19 of the 21 missions built by Spanish Franciscan priests in California during the late 1700s through early 1800s. Padre Junipero Serra usually is credited with founding California's missions, but Padre Estevan Tapis established Mission Santa Inés on September 17, 1804. Construction on the church was completed in 1807; it was partially destroyed by an earthquake in 1812. The mission has been in continuous use since 1817. Today Mission Santa Inés has an active parish. Mass is said daily. On Sundays, there are several celebrations of Mass in English and Spanish.

The purpose of the mission system was to colonize California. The first step was to forcefully convert the native population to Christianity. Coerced labor built a self-sustaining village, and remnants of the *lavanderia* (water system) and other architectural bones are still standing. For example, some of the original walls, floor, tiles, along with the copper baptismal font and murals are still part of the church. Bells were an important part of mission life. Two from the collection of bells from the mission's early days are tolled at different times of the day.

Every year more than 100,000 visitors tour the grounds and buildings. The museum houses artifacts telling bits and pieces of the different people of the area: Indians, Spanish, Mexicans, and other early settlers. The museum collection includes oil paintings, silverwork, and wood carvings from the 17th and 18th centuries. There are also arrowheads, pestles and mortars, pottery, adobe bricks, pieces of the first altar, crucifixes, candlesticks, and musical instruments. In a separate special collection is a vestment that was worn by Padre Junipero Serra.

A National Landmark, Mission Santa Inés is the site of the first vineyards in the area, and also served as the first college and seminary in California. On the east side of the mission is an outdoor promenade with the 14 Stations of the Cross. The cemetery has 1,700 unmarked Indian graves and 75 marked graves of early California settlers. A rose garden and a boxwood hedge in the shape of a Celtic cross are popular attractions at the mission.

The gift shop carries Catholic gifts and a complete line of devotional items. The bookstore sells the "mission project packet" to accompany California schools fourth-grade curriculum.

Tours are self-guided—an audio tour is available to rent. The last tour starts at 4:30 p.m. Not much time is needed to cover all the sites of the museum, a few hours should be more than enough. ($)

SOLVANG VINTAGE MOTORCYCLE MUSEUM

(320 Alisal Rd. ☎ 805.686.9522 ⬤ motosolvang.com) Housed in a former outlet mall, this museum showcases a private collection of motorcycles, including rare and vintage pieces. The oldest bikes date back to the 1900s. Enthusiasts will recognize the names of AJS, BMW, Ducati, Gilera, Matchless, Moto Guzzi, Triumph, Velocette, and Vincent. Bikes are rotated and the displays change monthly. Open weekends and by appointment during the week. ($)

There is a sense of pride among Solvang innkeepers that their guest rooms are different from others, and not cookie cutter.

Lodging

With a few exceptions, lodging in Solvang is clustered in the Village, which makes most places to stay convenient to most main attractions and sights. Almost all the lodging establishments are independently owned. This means a live person will answer the phone in Solvang and be able to take a reservation. Some reservations can be made online via an accommodation's website, or with other well-known travel websites such as hotels.com and other travel sites.

There is a sense of pride among Solvang innkeepers that their establishment's rooms are different from others, and not cookie cutter. Rooms within one hotel come in different sizes and have varying décor. Rather than using room numbers, many places name the rooms thematically, for example, after flowers, trees, or wines.

Unless otherwise noted, air conditioning, Internet access, complimentary coffee, complimentary continental breakfast, ice machine, television, and a pool are standard amenities. Given Solvang's bevy of bakeries, expect that the breakfast will have fresh pastries from a nearby establishment. Don't settle for packaged goods shipped in from far away.

There are a fair number of old-school, reasonably priced motels to afford a low-priced getaway in Solvang. A new crop of boutique hotels that are a better fit with the wine country than with the Danish Capital of America have also arrived. Summer, weekends, and holidays are busy times for Solvang. Book early if wanting to visit then, and expect to pay top dollar.

Prices: Lodging in Solvang runs the gamut from "basic bed & a bath" to high-end luxury. Prices in this section are per night and broken into $$$ ($150 and over), $$ ($81 to $150) and $ ($80 or less). These figures represent low-to-peak-season rate ranges. The establishments are categorized by price range. Under each price breakout the listings are alphabetical.

BUDGET BUSTERS AND WORTH EVERY DIME

Go ahead and make it a special night. Expect the detailed touches and indulge. Given that the room is more expensive, stay around and enjoy it. Lie in bed for a while and feel that Egyptian cotton. Use up the high-end toiletries. Linger over the view.

ALISAL GUEST RANCH & RESORT

(1450 Alisal Rd. ☎ 805.688.6411 ⏺ alisal.com) If wishes were horses, then everyone would be riding at the Alisal Guest Ranch & Resort. The ranch harkens back to a rustic, gentler time when the moneyed and/or famous made getaways and spent their time reading, horseback riding, swimming, or fishing. They continue that tradition at the Alisal today, whiling away their time in the same way in the same beautiful setting.

A hotel since 1946, the 10,500-acre working cattle ranch offers 73 accommodations in studio rooms, deluxe studios, and two-room suites. In keeping with the underlying theme of "disconnect to reconnect," there are no phones or televisions in the rooms (phones, television, and Internet access are available on site). There is no air conditioning to combat summer's high heat, either.. Wood-burning fireplaces and plenty of oak firewood warm up the big, spacious rooms. Pendleton blankets complete the rustic ranch feel. The pool is heated all year long, and the children's activity center is open daily. The golf course and lake are reserved for guests only, as are the dining rooms. There is a cocktail lounge and snack bar for drinks and food not covered by the room rate.

The idea is to not leave The Alisal after checking in. Why would one? Other activities include horseback riding, archery, fishing, boating, billiards, and ping-pong. Plus, there's a fitness center, spa, and library.

The Alisal, as it is known locally, is named for the Chumash word, *alisal*, for "grove of sycamores," and it shares a property line with the Ronald Reagan Ranch. Amenities are for guests only. There is a two-night minimum stay. Many families have long-standing traditions of enjoying The Alisal, particularly during holidays. (A Thanksgiving trail ride and a Christmas morning hike are memory makers.) Reservations, which can be hard to come by, are a must. ($$$)

CHUMASH CASINO RESORT
(3400 E. Highway 246, Santa Ynez ☎ 800.248.6274
⬤ ChumashCasino.com) Three months after opening in 2004, the 106-room Chumash Casino Resort earned a AAA Four-Diamond Award. Each year since, the hotel has received the same distinction. Housed in a separate building from the casino, the quiet hotel features spacious, elegantly appointed guest rooms overlooking the bucolic Santa Ynez Valley countryside. Large, beautifully detailed paintings of tribal ancestors hang in the lobby that welcomes guests. Located on the lobby level, the Business Center offers high-speed Internet access, copy and fax machines, and computers for guest use.

The Fitness Center has a variety of popular fitness and exercise machines, including treadmills, elliptical trainers, and the like. Premium guest rooms have a balcony, small seating area, deep-seated bathtub and shower combination, a safe, and luxury robes. There is complimentary turn-down service, too. Reservations are recommended. ($$$)

HADSTEN HOUSE INN & SPA
(1450 Mission Dr. ☎ 805.688.3210 🖰 hadstenhouse.com)
Hadsten House is an excellent example of taking a tired old property and revitalizing it into something exciting and new—in a way that raises the bar for other lodging in the area. The décor is sophisticated and elegant yet maintains a homey, comfortable feel. Detailed touches include full turn-down service nightly with a little bedside gift, and there's also room service. Not to mention high-thread-count sheets, custom bedding, LCD television with DVD players, and refrigerators in each room. Room rates include full American breakfast, and wine and cheese reception from 3 to 5 p.m. daily. The restaurant, open for dinner only, is open to nonguests, too. Massage, facials, body treatments, and waxing are available at the on-site **Haven Day Spa**. ($$$)

HOTEL CORQUE ✪ Must See!
(400 Alisal Rd. ☎ 805.688.8000 🖰 hotelcorque.com) Upscale—and a taste of Solvang on the upswing—Hotel Corque is a premium boutique hotel owned by the Santa Ynez Band of Chumash Indians. Situated on the edge of the Village, Hotel Corque took over the former Royal Scandinavian, completely gutted it, and created a destination spot. There are 122 rooms, 16 of them suites. The Chairman's Suite takes up 1,200 feet

on the top floor. (The Chumash tribal leader is referred to as the chairman.) Each room has pampering touches, such as Egyptian cotton sheets and plush robes. A huge outdoor pool, Jacuzzi, and covered patio help extend that luxurious feel. Wood sculptures and photographs of horses accent the interior. Seating in the lobby invites a rest. There is no room service, but take-out is available from the popular and always busy **Root 246**, which is part of the Hotel Corque compound. The first floor business center offers Internet access, computers, a copier, and fax machine. There is no fitness center, but guests receive a pass to one nearby that offers equipment and classes. If you can't get a reservation, at least come in and take a look around. The name? In keeping with the wine country theme, it is a play on the word *cork*.

PETERSEN VILLAGE INN ✪ Must See!

(1576 Mission Dr. ☎ 805.688.3121 ☗ peterseninn.com) A *AAA Four Diamond* rated accommodation. This family-owned and run business was built by the patriarch, Earl Petersen, an architect responsible for much of the design of Solvang. The feel is Old World comfort and security—four-poster beds, fluffy bedding, and comfortable sitting areas. Each of the 40 rooms is a tad different in design, because Petersen first designed the building around a courtyard, then he divided the building into rooms. The view from some of the rooms overlooks Copenhagen Drive and gives a village-like feel. The deluxe tri-level Tower suite offers a fireplace and Jacuzzi tub. Two conference rooms are available on the ground floor. Two cafés and more than a dozen fine shops make up the "village." Modified room rates allow for including dinner at the on-site dining room. The breakfast buffet is a step up from the standard continental breakfast. There is no pool. Plentiful covered parking. ($$$)

KEEPING IT WITHIN THE FAMILY BUDGET

With a little research, good timing, and a bit of luck you can score great lodging at a great price. Conversely, some of these middle-priced rooms may not have the latest in television technology but there will be cable and a remote. There is a good chance the establishment will have a vestige of vintage Roadside Vernacular architecture, such as a windmill or a Viking ship on the roof. Good accommodations for a fair price.

HAMLET MOTEL

(1532 Mission Dr. ☎ 805.688.4413 ☗ hamletmotel.com) This 15-room classic motel (the parking space is right in front of the guest room) is undergoing some cosmetic changes. The bones of the place won't be moved around though. The complimentary continental breakfast is across the street at **Olsen's Danish Village Bakery**. There is one suite and its upstairs location gives a bird's-eye view to busy Mission Drive. Amenities include ice machine, cable television, refrigerators, and a gazebo, which is soon to be turned into a deck. The footprint of the motel is small, but the rooms and bathrooms are spacious. Bathrooms have windows—not always easy to find nowadays. There is no pool. ($$)

HOLIDAY INN EXPRESS

(1455 Mission Dr. ☎ 805.688.2018 ☗ hiexpress.com) This American classic stands sentry at the beginning of the Solvang "strip." The updated 82 rooms are spacious and quiet. Many of them overlook **Hans Christian Andersen Park**. The on-site outdoor pool is small, and the complimentary full American breakfast is big. Underground parking is welcome in the hot Solvang summer. ($$)

KING FREDERIK INN

(1617 Copenhagen Dr. ☎ 805.688.5515 🖱 kingfrederikinn.com)
The address reads Copenhagen Drive, but you can enter from Mission Drive. This 46-room inn has a heated pool, Jacuzzi, and continental breakfast in the lobby. The central location can't be beat, particularly if tickets to **Theaterfest** are involved. ($$)

WINE COUNTRY MANOR

(1440 Mission Dr. ☎ 805.688.2383
🖱 **Winecountrymanor.com)** This is the first windmill to welcome visitors arriving in Solvang from the west. An idle, baby grand piano greets guests in the lobby. Formerly known as the Kronborg Inn, the nonsmoking, 39-room hotel's recent remodel is evident in the flat-screen televisions, the contemporary colors, and sumptuous linens and matching drapes. Each room has wi-fi, cable television, ironing board and irons, hair dryers, and a refrigerator. Suites feature hot tubs. The complimentary continental breakfast includes eggs and waffles. ($$)

MEADOWLARK INN

(2644 Mission Dr. ☎ 805.688.4631
🖱 **meadowlarkinnsolvang.com)** Located outside the Village, the Meadowlark Inn says wine country rather than Denmark. Situated on two acres of a park-like setting, the inn's 18 rooms are categorized by wine type, for example, the Chardonnay

is a standard king with hot tub. The Cabernet is the garden king suite, and the large private garden comes complete with hot tub, fire pit, and hammock. Fireplaces and Jacuzzi vary by room. A kitchenette room is available. All rooms come with wi-fi, television, coffee maker, and refrigerator. A DVD library, books, and games are available. A light breakfast is included in the room charge. The inn's rooms are laid out horseshoe style with a beautiful center garden framed by oak and redwood trees. A gazebo, picnic tables, fire ring, comfy Adirondack chairs, flowers, and blooms accent the center lawn. A small swimming pool sits across the driveway. There are some accommodations for pets, but reservations must be made in advance. The property is popular for events such as small weddings and family reunions. Snowbirds like the weekly and monthly rentals. The on-site owners are wine experts and lead tasting tours. ($$/$$$)

MIRABELLE INN & RESTAURANT

(409 First St. ☎ 805.688.1703 ⬤ solvanginns.com) Like something from a Hans Christian Andersen fairy tale, the vine-covered Mirabelle Inn has 11 romantic rooms furnished with antiques and fireplaces. Some of them have whirlpool tubs. The signature of the Mirabelle is its personal touch, such as the nightly turn-down service. There are two sitting rooms and books, games, and DVDs are available for guests to relax. The inn is located on the edge of the Village, which gives it a secluded and get-away-from-it-all feel. (The heart of the Village with the bakeries, shops, restaurants, tasting room, and other businesses is only two blocks away.) Massage, body treatments, and other spa services are available on site. The room charge includes a full breakfast, afternoon wine and appetizers, and evening treats. The on-site restaurant, **Mirabelle Restaurant**, is open to the public for dinner Thursday through Sunday. Ask about wine tours and small events. The proprietors also own the Meadowlark Inn and are noted food and wine experts. There is no pool. ($$/$$$)

Lodging

ROYAL COPENHAGEN INN
(1579 Mission Dr. ☎ 805.688.5561 🖱 royalcopenhageninn.com)

The check-in office of the two-story Royal Copenhagen Inn may look vaguely familiar, that is if one has visited the town hall of Ebeltoft, Mols, Denmark. The Danish-owned inn is built to look like a village from the old country and each guest room has a different façade. Room choices are loft (the bed is in an open area upstairs), suite, king, queen, and two queens. There is also a large executive suite with a surprisingly sizeable kitchen, living room, and bedroom. The bathroom has a coin-free washer and dryer. There are extra charges for roll-away beds, cribs are no extra charge. Nine of the inn's 49 rooms are designated as pet friendly; check with office before making reservations. Other amenities include a conference room, a secret garden in back, heated pool and barbecue area, wi-fi, and complimentary continental breakfast. Those wanting to soak in a bathtub should look elsewhere; there are only showers in the bathrooms. ($$/$$$)

SOLVANG GRDNS BOUTIQUE COUNTRY INN ✪ Must See!
(293 Alisal Rd. ☎ 805.688.4404 🖱 Solvanggardens.com)

Beautiful Solvang Gardens Boutique Country Inn lays claim to being the first motel in Solvang. Built in 1950, the 24-room property is on the edge of the Village and sought after for its privacy and serenity. There is no outdoor pool or outdoor Jacuzzi—visitors book rooms here because of the gardens.

Solvang Gardens Boutique Country Inn is a certified green property, the first in Santa Barbara County. Along with their commitment to the environment, the on-site, hands-on owners and managers do a lot of the upgrades and remodeling themselves. Amenities vary by room. King suites are huge. Bigger than many apartments, they come with a kitchen, living room, and bedroom. Other features include whirlpool tubs, fireplaces, marble bathrooms, and kitchenettes. Detail touches like intricately carved room doors and the cute breakfast room accent the property. (They don't build them like this anymore.) Breakfast is bigger than most continental ones served in town. The large garden in the rear is rented out for weddings and private events. Shady fruit trees shelter the lawn and a gurgling fountain lends an extra calm. There is also a spa cottage on site for massages and other treatments.

Celebrities and other recognizable names and faces stay here. Each year families return for holidays, reunions, and other traditions. Bicyclists love this place, too. All the rooms are nonsmoking, though smoking is allowed in the front garden. No pets. Weekly rates are available. ($$/$$$)

SVENDSGAARD'S DANISH LODGE
(1711 Mission Dr. ☎ 805.688.3277 🖱 svendsgaardslodge.com)
Scandinavian-owned Svendsgaard's may be past its prime but the three-story structure continues to maintain a commanding presence at the eastern gateway to the Village. The stone turret-like entrance to the office leads to the large lobby where continental breakfast, which includes fresh pastries from a

bakery down the street, is served. The rooms are large. There are two-room suites and deluxe suites with kitchenettes and dining areas are available. Some of the 48 rooms/suites have fireplaces and balconies overlooking the Jacuzzi and large pool that is heated March through October. Svendsgaard's could use some tender loving care and basic upkeep. No pets are allowed. ($/$$$)

WINE VALLEY INN

(1564 Copenhagen Dr. ☎ 805.688.2111 winevalleyinn.com)
Bright, white, and tucked away on the west end of Copenhagen Drive, the Wine Valley Inn has 68 rooms, which include suites and cottages. The landscaped courtyards have koi ponds. ($$/$$$)

HEY, WE GOT IT FOR UNDER BUDGET

The price is better than right, and the place is clean. Maybe there won't be a goose down comforter on the bed, but it doesn't get that cold here anyway. Pocket the savings or spend another night? You decide.

SOLVANG INN & COTTAGES

(1518 Mission Dr. ☎ 805.688.4702 🔖 solvanginn.com) The gossip bench, *sladerbænken* in Danish, and Bob, the life-size Viking wood carving next to it, invite weary travelers to rest in one of the 44 rooms. Some of those rooms are really stand-alone cottages. Solvang Inn & Cottages is a simple mom and pop place; mom and pop just happen to be from Denmark. The rooms are basic and clean. There is one family unit that sleeps up to six with two bedrooms and one bath. Monthly rates are available and snowbirds take advantage of the roomy cottages during the winter. These homes away from homes have a kitchen, gas fireplace, and living room. Continental breakfast is served at the bakery across the street. There is a heated pool, Jacuzzi, wi-fi, cable, ice, and complimentary coffee. No pets are allowed. ($/$$)

VIKING MOTEL

(1506 Mission Dr. ☎ 805.688.1337 ✆ vikingmotelsolvang.com) This 13-room motel was built in 1920 by Danish immigrants. This is the type of place for people who say, "What? I just need a place to lay my head. Why pay so much?" Each of the Spartan rooms comes with air conditioning, microwave, fridge, and television. The tables with umbrellas on the lawn around the fountain are a good place to relax after a day exploring. The owner/managers are friendly and helpful. There is no pool. There are pet rooms available. ($/$$)

RV PARKS AND CAMPING

Though technically not in Solvang, there is an RV campground in Buellton, the town next to Solvang. RVs are welcome to park for free in Solvang during the day at the Veterans Memorial Hall, 1745 Mission Drive, directly across from Mission Santa Inés. The two closest traditional campgrounds are about a 15- to 20-minute car ride away.

FLYING FLAGS RV PARK

(180 Avenue of the Flags, Buellton ☎ 877.783.5247 flyingflags. com) Flying Flags RV Park sits next to Highway 101. RVs feel right at home at any of the 260 sites. Along with the grassy pull-throughs and hook ups, amenities include wi-fi, cable television, fitness center, laundry facilities, playground, and an on-site store. No RV? Cottages are available for rent. ($/$$)

CACHUMA LAKE RECREATION AREA
(2225 Highway 154 ☎ 805.686.5050 🖱 countyofsb.org)
Cachuma provides more than 400 sites for tent, trailer, and RV camping. One hundred of those sites come with full electrical, water, and sewer hookups. Camping is on a first come, first served basis. One- or two-bedroom cabins with bathrooms and kitchenettes, fully equipped trailers, and yurts can be reserved. There are also group campsites accommodating from 32 to 120 people. ($)

GAVIOTA STATE PARK
(10 Refugio Beach Rd. ☎ 805.968.1033 🖱 parks.gov.ca) Located 11 miles south on Highway 101, there are 40 campsites in this seaside campground. The price for the multimillion dollar views of the ocean and the Channel Islands is charged in the frequent high winds that roar through the campground. There is a trailhead leading to Gaviota Peak, which offers a bird's-eye view of the Pacific Ocean and the islands. Fishermen and boaters make good use of the pier on the west side of the campground. The beach scene in *Sideways* was filmed here. ($)

The Village streets are filled with imported Danish treasures such as handmade lace, music boxes, jewelry, kitchen accessories, and arts and crafts.

Shopping

With more than 150 independently owned and unique retail outlets, Solvang is a major shopping destination. The Village streets are filled with imported Danish treasures such as hand-made lace, music boxes, jewelry, kitchen accessories, and arts and crafts. It's not all about Denmark, however. There are many specialty shops featuring domestic and homegrown goods, too. The number of shopping opportunities are too numerous for the scope of this book, so establishments featuring customary home furnishing and standard items found easily in any shopping environment have been omitted. You will discover them while exploring the 2.2-square mile Village. So be sure to stop in and look around. There is plenty to buy. Solvang also has a handful of thrift, secondhand, and consignment stores. Their mishmash of inventory tells a different Solvang story, so don't overlook paying them a visit. Another great thing about patronizing independently owned and often family-run businesses is the pride of ownership that shows itself in attentive service. Plus the folks manning the place are happy to have you in their shop. Unless otherwise noted, businesses are open daily, typically from 10 a.m. to 5 or 6 p.m. Shops are usually closed on Christmas and New Year's Day.

THAT TOUCH OF DENMARK

Most likely the reason for visiting Solvang is for a dose of the Danish thing, which happens to be much more than aebleskiver and windmill refrigerator magnets. The streets of Solvang are filled with top-quality handicrafts, décor and embellishments, fine foodstuffs, and other authentic goods.

THE BOOK LOFT ⊗ Must See!

(1680 Mission Dr. ☎ 805.688.6010 🖱 bookloftsolvang.com)
Run by book lovers for book lovers, the Book Loft has been a Solvang favorite for more than 40 years. A full-service bookstore catering to all ages and reading levels, it also hosts book signings, poetry readings, and other special events. In addition to a full range of books and magazines, The Book Loft carries a large selection of Scandinavian literature in English and in several Scandinavian languages. There's also a good collection of books by local authors, games, and puzzles. Upstairs, where the **Hans Christian Andersen Museum** makes its home, is the used book department; for the serious bibliophile there is an antiquarian section. Don't worry about lugging all the books home, shipping is available. Gift wrapping is too.

EDELWEISS

(1692 Copenhagen Dr. ☎ 805.686.4671 🖱 edelweissgifts.com)
Just in case you forgot to pick up a pretty little something at the shop around the corner, there's Edelweiss. The well-stocked shelves hold plenty of delicate gifts and items for the home. Collectible dolls and jewelry are popular items. Edelweiss opens at 8:30 a.m. and closes at 9 p.m.

ELNA'S DRESS SHOP

(1673 Copenhagen Dr. ☎ 805.688.4525) The original owner, Elna, has retired. Most of the inventory is contemporary clothing and accessories now, but a corner of the dress shop is dedicated to handmade Danish costumes. Elna's Dress Shop has been in the same location since 1942—in the heart of the Village. It has retained its Ol' Solvang ambiance and now serves second- and third-generation customers looking for an authentic outfit.

FAMILY COATS OF ARMS

(473 Atterdag Rd. ☎ 805.688.7660 🖲 familycoatsofarms.com)
Maybe all this Danish pride in Solvang has instilled a desire to research the family tree. How deep down do those roots go? This is the place to find out. The Family Coats of Arms specialty is European names. Embroidered coats of arms are popular, as are the bronze shields, steins, mugs, and rings. The research on name histories is through a computer database, which can give a name's origin and references in history.

GAVEAESKEN

(433 Alisal Rd. ☎ 805.686.5699) The shape of the shop Gaveaesken, also known as the Giftbox, looks like a jewelry box. It is small, cozy, and full of pretty, dainty, and shiny items. Gaveaesken features domestic and European, with the emphasis on Scandinavian fine gifts. There is a requisite lineup of blue and white Solvang-inscribed bells, windmills, and other souvenirs near the entrance.

GERDA'S IRON ART

(1676 Copenhagen Dr. ☎ 805.688.3750) The door to Gerda's is the kind cut in half and the top part is open (a *Dutch door*). It is an enticing sight from the sidewalk: the inventory of handcrafted wrought iron, brass gifts, and copper items neatly arranged in rows and stacks. Lace curtains, teapots, cups and saucers, and wine gift items lend a soft touch to the display. There's also a huge supply of blue and white souvenir plates, knickknacks, and bric-a-brac. Going through the stock at Gerda's can be fun.

HANSON'S CLOCK SHOP & JEWELERS

(467 Alisal Rd. ☎ 805.688.5211 ☋ clocksclocks.com) The chorus of ticktocks and cuckoos heard outside the store is from all the clocks inside Hanson's Clock Shop. In addition to cuckoos, Hanson's has all kinds of timepieces from around the globe. (They do repairs, too.) Open since 1969, the third generation, family-run store has jewelry, crystal items, and a selection of other fine imported gifts. Hanson's is also a trusted source for repairing clocks.

KATRINA'S TRINKET SHOP

(1653 Copenhagen Dr. ☎ 805.688.9565) In addition to the standard stuff one would find in any tourist town, for example, T-shirts, key chains, and fridge magnets, Katrina's carries emergency-type items such as one-use cameras.

NODDING PLACE QUILT & GIFT BOUTIQUE

(1662 Copenhagen Dr. ☎ 805.688.4858) There are not many better things than nodding off to sleep tucked under a handmade quilt? At the Nodding Place it might be a little difficult to choose only one quilt from the rows and rows of choices available. There are seasonal quilts, festive ones, and other theme-based quilts. Accompanying home accessories and accents along with kitchen goods fill the shelves, too. The store has a bright, warm, and colorful feel.

RASMUSSEN'S ✪ Must See!

(1697 Copenhagen Dr. ☎ 805.688.6636 🖱 rasmussenssolvang. com) Situated on the corner of Copenhagen and Alisal, Rasmussen's is the retail anchor of Solvang. The 5,000-square-foot department store carries a complete line of Scandinavian goods. There are books, stationery, kitchen tools, food items, linens, ornaments, and playthings. The selection of needle-work, fabric, and yarns is worth a look, too. To make things easier for some, there is a gift registry.

NORDIC KNIVES

(1634 Copenhagen Dr., #C ☎ 805.688.3612 🖱 nordicknives.com) There are a lot more knives here than just the fancy kitchen ones. There are cases and cases of sport knives under lock and key. Nordic Knives specializes in custom made knives and carries Randall, Chris Reeve, and William Henry knives, among others. For those wanting to sell a knife or collection, Nordic Knives sells on consignment or purchases directly.

PEBBLE PEOPLE

(1608 Copenhagen Dr. ☎ 805.688.7616 🖱 pebblepeople.com) Look for the big sign that says "Old World Clocks and Music Boxes" on the outside of the building because it isn't easy to spot the smaller Pebble People one. This shop has an amazing inventory of all types of clocks, music boxes, and jewelry. Keep moving past the rows and rows of tall glass cases filled with high-quality, handcrafted items. There is another room filled with merchandise. Proud of their customer service, Pebble People has been a family-owned business since 1972.

ROYAL COPENHAGEN SHOP

(1683 Copenhagen Dr. ☎ 805.688.6660
🖱 royalcopenhagenshop.com) This pretty store carries a lot more than delicate jewelry, crystal, collector plates, and figurines. There are contemporary housewares and kitchen tools, too. You'll find porcelain here you can't find out of Denmark. Wool sweaters, goose down comforters, and pillows provide that authentic arctic feel of Scandinavia. For the genuine feel of Denmark, this is the shop where Danish is spoken by the staff, who all happen to be family.

SOLVANG ANTIQUE CENTER ✪ Must See!

(486 First St. ☎ 805.686.2322 🖱 solvangantiques.com) It is fitting that antique center's entrance is underneath the world-famous chiming carillon clock tower because clocks in all permutations line the stairs and walls. The center boasts having the largest selection of fine antique clocks and watches in the country. The multiple-dealer—there are 65—gallery specializes in 18th and 19th century European and American furniture. Additionally, jewelry, dishes, art, and accessories fill the store. This is not a dusty, funky antique shop but rather more of a museum with loving curators.

ARLENE'S BASEMENT

(486 First St. ☎ 805.688.6222 🖱 solvangantiques.com) This new venture of the **Solvang Antique Center**'s owners is located, appropriately enough, in the basement level of the same building. The inventory at Arlene's includes contemporary items as well as antiques. Hours vary.

SOLVANG SHOE STORE

(1663 Copenhagen Dr. ☎ 805.688.4065 🖱 solvangshoe.com) This is the shop with the huge red clog in front of it. Toward the rear of the store is the Cloggery, where a large selection of the clunky looking, good-for-your-feet-and-back shoes sits. There is also a collection of pretty painted clogs. Dansko, Sven, and Bastad are some of the clogs' brand names. Solvang Shoe Store carries footwear that is intended for use, not just show. Think sneaker, not stiletto. There is a large selection of walking shoes such as Mephisto, Clarks, and Ecco. Open daily.

THE JULE HUS

(1580 Mission Dr. ☎ 805.688.6601 🖱 solvangchristmashouse. com) The yuletide celebration is year-round at The Jule Hus. Any time is the right to buy some tree ornaments or other hallmarks of the season. The Christmas decorations span imported delicate, hand-blown glass bulbs to wooden folk art crosses. The theme is Santa-centric in the store, but there are nativity scenes, advent wreaths, and other evidence of Christmas being Christian in origin for sale, too. The Jule Hus provides insight into Scandinavian Christmas traditions and how the holiday is celebrated. Closed on Christmas.

FOR KIDS ONLY

Solvang is known as a family-friendly destination. Nothing says this louder and more clearly than the number of stores dedicated to children. Solvang's children's shops can be broken into two general categories: clothing and toys.

ATTERDAG KIDS

(447 Atterdag Rd. ☎ 805.686.4074 ☉ atterdagkids.com) Call it couture for kids. Atterdag Kids is dedicated to dressing babies through young teens in the latest fashions. The vast array of styles and colors represents a wide range of designers and brand names, all of high quality.

JUNE BUG

(485 Alisal Rd., #137 ☎ 805.693.4433
☉ myjunebugbaby.com) Don't be fooled by the beautiful interior and baby-soft goods. June Bug is on a mission. With a commitment to provide sustainable products made from organic materials, the store carries inventory that is safe for babies, children, and grownups, as well as the environment. Besides clothes and toys, all the staples for setting up a nursery are also available. The target market is newborn to 4T.

KID'S CLUB

(1688 Copenhagen Dr. ☎ 805.693.0075) A model car collection on glass shelves greets shoppers at the entrance, which is to the left as you look through the huge picture window from the sidewalk. Inside the store are real kid-size cars for cruising sidewalks. Other toys are interspersed throughout the clothing inventory. Kid's Club carries lots of soft, teeny-tiny infant wear.

MARMALADE SKY

(2023 Mission Dr. ☎ 805.686.5208) Primarily a clothing store for young children, this sun-drenched shop has a few toys and other playthings accenting the merchandise displays. The durable clothing is colorful, fun, and comfortable. Kids may not find Marmalade Sky an enjoyable retail experience, but their fashion-minded parents and indulgent grandparents will.

NATHALIE'S DOLLHOUSE

(1693 Copenhagen Dr. ☎ 805.688.6533) The wide selection of miniature doll houses and furniture is enchanting but that's not the only reason to visit this 3,000 square-foot emporium. There is an emphasis on no-battery-needed and nonelectric toys. Windup toys, steam engines, submarines, boats, books, dolls of all makes, shapes, and sizes, plus lots more.

SOLVANG CHILDREN'S SHOP

(1666 Copenhagen Dr. ☎ 805.688.6218 solvangdresses.com) Looking for a child's Danish outfit in the Old World style? This is the place. Here it is called a "Solvang Dress." There is contemporary children's clothing, too. Grandparents love this shop. Solvang Dresses are available through their website, too.

SOLVANG TOYLAND

(1664 Copenhagen Dr. ☎ 805.688.7577 🖱 solvangtoyland.com) Solvang Toyland is an emporium of fun for kids. This place is bursting! Filled to the rafters with toys, games, puzzles, books, magic sets, dolls, model cars and planes, and balls, this store has something for everyone no matter what their age. Boxes, shelves, and pockets spill over with fun. But wait, there's more—it is not just about playing around. Fancy collectibles make their temporary home here, too, as do educational playthings.

FABRICS AND FIBERS

Solvang and spinning wheels go together. Other textile arts and crafts are a natural fit with the Danish Capital of America, too. Looms, a mound of wool from freshly shorn sheep, and nimble fingers cross-stitching at a furious pace show an appreciation for a talent not practiced much anymore.

ELVERHØJ MUSEUM STORE

(1624 Elverhoy Way ☎ 805.686.1211 ✆ elverhoj.org) The museum's gift store has an excellent selection of finished textile handicrafts and the supplies and tools necessary to create them. There are Danish ornament craft kits. In the vintage corner, needlepoint items are available. Swedish fine woven textiles and linens are part of the gift item selection. Ornaments handcrafted by museum docents are for sale, too. Check the museum's class schedule for lace making classes.

THUMBELINA

(1683-A Copenhagen Dr. ☎ 805.688.4136 ✆ thumbelina.com) This specialty store carries European and Danish embroidery supplies. Thumbelina also has kits, needles, thread, bell-pulls, and more. Store service includes helping to hunt down hard-to-find items. To go along with its fairy tale name, Thumbelina is housed in the H.C. Andersen Hus, a model of the story-teller's Denmark home.

SOLVANG NEEDLEWORK

(1578 Mission Dr. ☎ 805.688.6151) Solvang Needlework is located in **Petersen Village**. Its imported and domestic embroideries, fabrics, and supplies are for perfect for cross-stitch and needlepoint. There's a lot of inventory in this shop, so make sure time allows for sifting through it. The prices are fair and the staff is helpful and friendly.

VILLAGE SPINNING AND WEAVING ✪ Must See!

425 B Alisal Rd. ☎ 805.686.1192 🌐 villagespinweave.com)
Village Spinning and Weaving carries equipment, books, and supplies for fiber artists, including tatters and bobbin lacers. The recently expanded store carries big items like spinning wheels and looms to small tools like bobbins and needles. Look for spinning wheels and loom demonstrations. Actually, they aren't formal demonstrations but rather artisans plying their craft. It is fun to watch.

ART SPACES AND GALLERIES

Though no one would describe the scene as thriving, the visual arts are alive in Solvang. Scattered around the Village is an eclectic mixture of outlets producing paintings, blown glass, jewelry, photographs, and more.

GERLACH PHOTOGRAPHY

(1539 Mission Dr. ☎ 805.688.1708 🌐 gerlachphoto.com) The beautiful nature scenes of the Santa Ynez Valley captured by the camera aren't the only ones hanging in this gallery. They are predominant, though, and stunning. Limited edition prints are available framed or matted in a large variety of sizes.

LITTLE PINE STUDIO

(439-B 2nd St. ☎ 805.895.5055 🌐 LittlePineStudio.com) Artist Deborah Dal Zuffo brings nature to life using watercolor, ink, pencil, pastel, and colored pencil drawings, and ceramics. Her "little" working art studio is filled with vibrant colors and meticulously rendered paintings inspired by local scenery. In addition to her original art, she also produces cards, mugs, and other gift items. Open Thursday through Sunday 11 a.m. to 5 p.m. or by appointment.

Shopping

PAVLOV ART GALLERY

(1608 Copenhagen Dr., Suite C ☎ 805.686.1080 📍 Pavlovgallery. com) This gallery features the work of artist Chris Pavlov, who moved from Europe to the United States in 2003, and other European and local artists. Contemporary, impressionistic, or expressionist in style, the paintings and sculptures in this gallery are bold, bright, and big. Pavlov Art Gallery provides a dramatic departure from Solvang's Old World Danish theme.

THE ARTISTIC PONY STUDIO, LTD.

(446 First St. ☎ 805.686.9899 📍 theartisticpony.com) Jeff and Sue Moualim, the owners of The Artistic Pony, aren't artists themselves, but created their space so they could promote the work of local artisans and craftsmen (and others from around the world). Traditional and eclectic pieces are featured in the store, such as gemstones, sterling silver, glass, pottery, and garden art. The loyal and strong base of local customers asked for classes. Now there are monthly workshops. Beading, precious metals, wire wrapping, gemology, pencil, fused glass, and Christmas ornaments are some past classes. Visitors are welcome to ask about a schedule. Limited hours.

WINDMILL GLASSWORKS, ETC.

(436 A Alisal Rd. ☎ 805.688.8722 🖱 windmillglassworks.com)
Enter right under the big windmill on Alisal near the post office. Pass by the large display of blue and white tchotchkes and souvenirs for some vivid, fantastical, and fun items. Toward the back are brilliantly colored pieces of glass art in a variety of sizes, forms, and functions. An excellent selection of glass jewelry entices the eye, too, as do the glass art clocks.

Z FOLIO GALLERY

(1685 Copenhagen Dr. ☎ 805.693.8480 🖱 zfolio.com) Along with specializing in Czech art glass, Z Folio Gallery has quite a portfolio of handmade jewelry from the United States and abroad. There is also glass art sculpture and functional pieces in vivid hues. Large nature photography decorates the walls. The gallery pieces are contemporary in style.

CLOTHES RACK

For the woman who could use some retail therapy, a shot in the arm so to speak, Solvang has the right prescription. From low-dosage casual wear to overdosing on high-end treats, there are a variety of shops to keep you covered. There are a few shops for men's apparel too.

BELLAGIO LADIES BOUTIQUE

(1511 Mission Dr. B ☎ 805.688.1005 🖱 bellagiosolvang.com)
Dressing Solvang women since 1990. Beautiful women's clothing, including lingerie, is Bellagio's stock in trade. There is a great selection of jewelry and shoes, too. The store carries Seven Jeans, Lucky Brand, and Cosabella, among other brands.

Bellagio is the sister store to **Backdoor Boardshop**, or maybe its mother. At any rate, they share the same roof. Bellagio stays open until 7 p.m. except on Sundays.

Shopping

BERENGARIA

(1676 Copenhagen Dr., Suite B ☎ 805.688.8326) This Copenhagen Drive shop sells both whimsical and elegant handbags. Other big sellers are beaded T-shirts and unique jackets. The stock includes travel-related items, too.

FIRST STREET LEATHER

1634 Copenhagen Dr. ☎ 805.688.5215 ● firststreetleather.com) Part of the Solvang retail scene since 1972, First Street Leather sells belts, handbags, hats, jackets, shoes, and wallets—all made of leather, naturally. The inventory of well-made merchandise is large, and the staff is very helpful. There are plenty of sale rack items to tempt the shoppers.

JENGER'S EXCLUSIVE, HAND PAINTED WOMEN'S CLOTHING

(485 Alisal Rd., #170 ☎ 805.688.9379) A little spot of retail art near Copenhagen Square. The handmade pieces include painted, beaded, and jeweled apparel. Limited hours.

PARTS UNKNOWN

(1662 Copenhagen Dr. ☎ 805.686.9000 ● partsunknown.com) Dubbed a "fashion adventure," Parts Unknown features clothes that are designed to give a feeling of adventure and travel. The demographic is upscale. Clothing for men is available also. Features brands like Brighton, Tommy Bahama, and UGG Australia.

SANTA BARBARA DENIM CO.

(1608 Copenhagen Dr. ☎ 805.688.5458) As the name implies, there is denim at this boutique, but there's a whole lot more, too. Casual tops, blouses, dresses, and pants dominate the inventory—plus bathing suits in season. There are some dress-up pieces, too. Good pickings on purses, wallets, and other accessories.

THE SOCK LOFT

(475 First St., Suite 2 ☎ 805.686.0135) This is sock heaven, or maybe it is someone's sock fetish on display. Literally, there are thousands of socks for sale. Socks for everyone: infants, children, teens, women, and men—all colors, shapes, sizes, and functions. Legwarmers and other dancewear are available. It's not all about socks, though. Shoelaces, flip-flops, jewelry, scarves, and other fashion accoutrement are stashed in The Sock Loft.

TRUE ADDICTION, WOMEN'S CLOTHING

(485 Alisal Rd., #152 ☎ 805.686.2868) Depending on the severity of the addiction, a lot of money could be spent here on the high-quality fashion, or one could stop at a couple of good buys on cute shirts. The merchandise is geared toward a younger crowd.

IN A CLASS ALL BY THEMSELVES

With over 150 retail establishments, there is bound to be a couple of shops that defy classification. These are fun to check out and, who knows, maybe that's where a real treasure is hidden.

MYSTIC MERCHANT

(1640 Copenhagen Dr. ☎ 805 .693.1424

🖱 mysticmerchantsolvang.com) This place rocks. There are amethyst geodes, jade, citrine (said to invite money) and other geological pieces to increase spirituality. Candles, incense, music, books, and statuary are some of the other spiritual pieces for sale. Come by and say "Hi" to Ernest, the large store cat patrolling the premises. The staff is friendly and knowledgeable.

SHELBI RANCH–HANS CHRISTIAN ANDERSEN SQUARE

(435 First St. ☎ 805.693.5000) The juxtaposition of faded store fronts with cowboy and Wild West themes housed in faux Danish architecture is confusingly head-scratching enough. Throw in a café with a menu resembling that of a school carnival from another era (hotdogs and Danish Custard milk-shakes for starters) and other oddball retail, and that makes Shelbi Ranch a "real trip" in addition to the trip to Solvang. Oddball it may be, but one would be hard pressed to find anywhere else in the state that sells fabric for 99 cents a yard. There are bolts and bolts and bolts of fabric waiting to be measured off. A lot of sewing notions are available, too.

SOLVANG INDIAN SHOP

(1618 Copenhagen Dr. ☎ 805.686.9619) The Solvang Indian Shop is situated right under the Hamlet Square windmill. The store has artwork, folk crafts, and educational items about the many Native American tribes in North America.

VALLEY BOOKS

(1582 Mission Dr. ☎ 805.688.7160 🖱 valleybooks.biz) Take a
load off and curl up in one of the comfy chairs. Refresh with
a cup of caffeine from the café or catch up on email with
the wi-fi. There is a computer to rent if necessary. Part of
Petersen Village shops, Valley Books is as much about the
experience of book loving as it is about the reading of books.
The independent seller has used books with a selection of new
ones, which are inspired by local customers and readers. The
café brews fair trade coffee. A small inventory of gift items,
some handmade ones, is for sale, too.

With the rare exception, chain restaurants are nonexistent in Solvang.

Dining

No one goes hungry in Solvang. Restaurants are serious business here. Like the retail shops, most of the restaurants are independently owned and/or family run. Bakeries and Danish restaurants are the backbone of the Village dining scene. In recent years, wine country cuisine, with its emphasis on farm-to-table freshness, has been stealing the spotlight from the all-you-can-eat smorgasbords. Years ago, chain restaurants were banned from Solvang; the local Domino's and Subway were grandfathered in.

Not all restaurants have a license to serve liquor, though beer and wine are plentiful. As is to be expected, wine lists are taken seriously and are boasting points. Wine storage, or cellars, is often made into part of an establishment's décor. Not surprisingly, the Scandinavian spirit *akvavit*, or aquavit, is popular in Solvang. Made from grain or potatoes, akvavit usually contains 40 percent alcohol by volume. Drink it "shot style" from a small glass in one gulp.

New restaurants continue to open in Solvang. These new establishments are leaning away from the Danish mom-and-pop eateries that built the town. They are tending toward sustainable, farm-to-table food or a specific ethnic cuisine.

A couple of tips: 1) Though Solvang rolls up its sidewalks early, relax. The **Chumash Café** (in the **Chumash Casino Resort**) is open 24 hours a day, seven days a week. 2) In drought-plagued California a glass of water isn't automatically poured for diners. You may have to ask for water.

Prices: By Santa Barbara County standards, and given the expected gouge in heavily touristed areas, Solvang restaurant prices are not too expensive. The pretax, pre-tip, and per person prices in this section are an average based on an entree with an appetizer or dessert and no alcohol. Prices in this section are broken into $$$ ($51 and over), $$ ($21 to $50), and $ (up to $20).

Divided by type of food, restaurants are listed in categories, then alphabetically. There isn't room to list all Solvang restaurants or give a shout-out to all the wonderful places in the Santa Ynez Valley. Establishments also go out of business and new ones pop up. So sniff around and see where your nose takes you. *Velbekomme!*

BEST BET BAKERIES

Given northern Europe's prominence in food history annals as the original developers of dairy farming, it's not surprising that many locals say the number one reason to visit Solvang is the bakeries, where butter is at its best. After all, in the United States, "Danish" refers to a sweet baked good usually paired with coffee. In Solvang, however, it is strictly an adjective. For example, there are Danish sausages, Danish sandwiches, Danish chocolates…well, you get the idea. In Solvang, the bakery butter rings, coffee cakes, kringles, strudels, and tubs of butter cookies are intended for sharing, but no one will notice, or at least will not comment, if they are not. As a cost-saving measure, some bakeries will use part margarine–part butter in their baking. Ask about the butter load before ordering to make sure.

DANISH MILL BAKERY

(1682 Copenhagen Dr. ☎ 805.688.5805 🖱 danishmillbakery.com)
This bakery is tidy and bright with a sweet aroma in the air.
Butter cookies and other Danish standards are the reasons for
the long lines. The coffee shop's lunch menu offers Danish
sandwiches and salads. ($)

ENJOY CUPCAKES

(1661 Mission Dr ☎ 805.451.0284 🖱 enjoycupcakes.com)
Decidedly not Old World Danish, this bakery specializes in
the all-American cupcake, but kicks it up with wine country
flavorings such as Syrah and other varietals. Cupcakes also pay
homage to the motherland with takeoffs on classic Danish
treats such as aebleskiver. The menu of baked goods changes
regularly. The retail space shares a roof with the Olive House,
though the décor and atmosphere are markedly different.
The cupcake side is pretty, pastel, and brightly lit, versus the
earthy vibe and tones at the **Olive House**. Enjoy Cupcakes is
as much about the fun atmosphere of cupcakes as it is about
having one. Open Thursday through Sunday. ($)

JUST BAKED!

(1555 Mission Dr. ☎ 805.686.0136) New to Solvang's bakery
scene, Just Baked! is a café, coffee bar, and bakeshop all rolled
into one. Just Baked! is not a "Danish" bakery. Bakery items
include cinnamon buns, croissants (all kinds), muffins, scones,
brownies, cookies, and little surprises like Rice Krispy treats.
Full hot breakfasts are available. Panini, sandwiches, and salads
are perfect for lunch or an early dinner. There's even a Wine
Taster's Box, which includes bruschetta, focaccia, prosciutto,

salami, and Brie cheese. Just Baked! is open from 7 a.m. to 7 p.m.

MORTENSEN'S DANISH BAKERY ✪ Must See!
(1588 Mission Dr. ☎ 805.688.8373
🖰 **greenhousesolvang/bakery.com)** Part of the Inn at Petersen Village and the former site of two doctors' offices, Mortensen's keeps it simple and stays focused on being a European bakery. No jalapeño bagels here! Cinnamon rolls, napoleons, custard-filled pastries, shortbread, butter cookies, coffee, and tea headline the menu. Order at the bakery case, grab a table, wait for drink to be served, and spend an extra minute enjoying every sip and bite. The blonde wood tabletops are spotlessly clean in this sunny site. ($)

OLSEN'S DANISH VILLAGE BAKERY ✪ Must See!
(1529 Mission Dr. ☎ 805.688.6314
🖰 **olsensdanishvillagebakery.com)** The most congested spot in Solvang just may be right in front of Olsen's bakery cases in the morning. The faithful arrive by the busloads and join the locals in line for a loaf of prize-winning bread, an almond custard kringle, cookies, or any of the other buttery delights. Clattering coffee cups and chattering customers add to the bustling atmosphere. The town's old-time Danes regularly gather in the afternoon for a coffee klatch. Olsen's Danish Village Bakery's pedigree dates back to 1890 in Denmark. ($)

SOLVANG BAKERY
(460 Alisal Rd. ☎ 805.688.4939 🖰 solvangbakery.com) Souvenirs and other gifts share shelf space with Solvang bakery standards like butter cookies, butter rings, and other pastries at

this 30-plus-year-old bakery. There is a small, connecting café serving light fare and coffee, the perfect accompaniment to a baked goody. Solvang Bakery also specializes in wedding cakes. ($)

DANISH DELIGHTS

For a style of cooking that developed in a cold climate, Danish food acclimated nicely to Solvang's Mediterranean climate. Its meat-and-potatoes approach is lightened a bit with a large variety of salads and vegetables at smorgasbords. Often in the United States, smorgasbord is synonymous with cheap or inexpensive eating, kind of like a college dormitory. However, a true *smorgasbord* is expensive and takes days to prepare. According to Danish cookbooks, the first course at a smorgasbord is fish, followed by salads and cold meats. The third plate is for hot dishes. Room is always saved for sweet treats.

Mention Solvang and a common response is "Did you have any aebleskiver?" *Aebleskiver* is the most famous and popular Danish food in Solvang. Impress the locals and don't say anything sounding like "*apple-skiver*"— it is pronounced *aye-bill-ski-ver*. Somewhere in between a golf ball and tennis ball in size and shape, aebleskiver fall into the dessert or treat category. Basically, they are similar to a waffle or pancake in taste, and commonly served with raspberry jam and powdered sugar. There are as many variations to aebleskiver as there are people making them, adding fruit or other sweets to the batter, smothering them with syrup. In Denmark aebleskiver are a special treat for holidays; in Solvang, they are an everyday thing. Aebleskiver cookware, with recipes, can be purchased at shops around the Village. Remember, say *"aye-bill-ski-ver"* not *"apple-skiver."*

Medisterpolse: Danish pork sausage.

Frikadeller: Not sweet like Swedish meatballs, frikadeller, the Danish national dish, are meatballs served with cabbage in white sauce.

Open-Face Sandwiches: Often considered Denmark's national dish, the open-face sandwich is comprised of two slices of well-buttered bread with an assortment of ingredients layered on each slice. The ingredients must completely cover the bread, and the higher the ingredients stack the better. An endless combination of ingredients makes the possible number of open-face sandwiches infinite. Common ingredients include cheeses, onion rings, eggs, salmon, lettuce, herring, ham, cold meats, liver paste, and so on. Eaten with a knife and fork.

BIT O'DENMARK

(473 Alisal Rd. ☎ 805.688.5426) Housed in one of Solvang's original buildings, Bit O'Denmark has copper tabletops and a large copper-top coffee machine behind the blue and white tiled bar. The dimly lit restaurant offers Danish, continental, and American standard fare on its lunch and dinner menus. There is a traditional smorgasbord. A popular menu item is the open-face sandwich for two. The servers at Bit O'Denmark are seasoned professionals. There is a full bar for cocktails. ($$)

GREENHOUSE CAFÉ

(487 Atterdag Rd. ☎ 805.688.8408 🍴 greenhousesolvang.com) The all-glass building looks like the Copenhagen of today, and the menu reflects that architectural choice. A self-described Nordic bistro, the Greenhouse Café offers breakfast, lunch, and dinner. There's a Danish breakfast, open-face sandwich with Havarti cheese and Danish sausage on pumpernickel bread, in addition to the typical American omelet suggestions. The sandwich menu gives a nod to local preferences with items such as chicken chipotle wraps. There is a selection of Nordic sandwiches, too, featuring Danish sausage and open-face shrimp sandwiches. There is no corkage fee for any bottle of local wine. The large patio overlooks Copenhagen Drive, perfect for people watching. ($$)

HEIDELBERG INN RESTAURANT AND BEER GARDEN

(1618 Copenhagen Dr. ☎ 805.688.6213

🖱 theheidelberginn.com) The pretty patio setting underneath a windmill can't be beat. The beer and meal choices highlight Danish and German favorites. Sausages from both countries have equal billing on the lunch menu, and a vegetarian option is also available. After 5 p.m. various schnitzel plates, including soup or salad, take center stage. Homemade desserts are German chocolate cake, German apple strudel, and aebleskiver. Tap beer is poured into glasses, steins, or pitchers. Local wines are available, too. Seasonal hours. ($$)

LITTLE MERMAID

(1546 Mission Dr. ☎ 805.688.6141) This is the place with the really cute, wood-carved sign. The cozy restaurant is pretty cute, too. A loyal following of visitors and overflow from Paula's Pancake House keep the place busy at breakfast. American standards and Danish traditional items are served at lunch and dinner. Aebleskiver is served, too. Open daily. ($$)

PAULA'S PANCAKE HOUSE

(1531 Mission Dr. ☎ 805.688.2867) Paula's is a busy, bustling place. Get there early because there probably will be a wait. Clad in Danish costumes, the friendly, efficient wait staff delivers breakfast and lunch orders fast and fresh. Wide as a pizza and thin as a dime, Paula's pancakes come in a variety of styles. In other parts of the world, the Danish pancakes are called crepes. Other breakfast items are standard American fare, such as omelets, bacon, oatmeal, and really good fresh orange juice made in front of customers. Lunch is soup, salads, burgers, and sandwiches. There is a large patio for dining alfresco. ($$)

RED VIKING RESTAURANT

(1684 Copenhagen Dr. ☎ 805.688.6610 ☗ theredvikingrestaurant. com) The Red Viking is open daily for breakfast, lunch, dinner, and aebleskiver. This is the place locals suggest to visitors looking for Danish food. The smorgasbord features hot and cold Danish specialties. There is an ala carte menu, too, and open-face sandwiches. American dishes include sandwiches, beef, lamb, pork, and chicken. The Red Viking is owned and operated by the same family as Olsen's Danish Village Bakery. There is a full bar. ($$)

SOLVANG RESTAURANT ✪ Must See!

(1672 Copenhagen Dr. ☎ 805.688.4645 ☗ solvangrestaurant.com) The "Must See" of this restaurant is the sidewalk window serving aebleskiver, Arne's Famous Aebleskiver to be exact. You can see them making the aebleskiver, too. It is easy to spot by the line of people waiting for their fresh fried ball of dough. Breakfast and lunch are served inside the Solvang Restaurant. The interior has some pretty decorative touches, such as fairy tale murals and crests from Danish villages. The setting of Solvang Restaurant was used in the movie *Sideways*. ($$)

VIKING GARDEN
(446-C Alisal Rd. ☎ 805.688.1250

🖱 vikinggardenrestaurant.com) A large outdoor seating area filled with bright red tables with umbrellas is a perfect place to sample the long list of draft beers. The prices are good, too. The food menu offers Danish and European standards (sausage, meatball, sauerkraut,), American favorites (hamburgers, Ruben sandwiches) and Mexican standbys (quesadillas, burritos). Going for the beer is the best bet. Open for breakfast and lunch. ($$)

AMERICAN ALL-STARS

Sometimes the only thing that will kill the hunger pains is a good hamburger or a perfect slice of pizza. A fresh, crisp garden salad wouldn't be bad either. Whatever the craving, Solvang has the comfort food covered.

BELGIAN CAFÉ
(1671 Copenhagen Dr. ☎ 805.688.6018) Cute and quaint are the perfect adjectives for this sparkling clean, red and white restaurant tucked away in the core of Copenhagen Drive. The Belgian in the name refers to the waffles. There is also French toast along with crepes to give it a European flair. The menu turns "red, white, and blue" with its lunch offerings of burgers,

sandwiches, and salads. Hearty American omelet breakfasts are also available. Serving breakfast and lunch. ($$)

BIG BOPPER DRIVE-IN

(1510 Mission Dr. ☎ 805.688.6018) You know how Solvang really isn't a part of Denmark, it just looks that way? Well, the Big Bopper Drive-In isn't really a 1950s burger joint; it just kind of looks that way. In the back parking lot is evidence that carhops may have skated here once, but that's about it for the drive-in part. If in Solvang when the urge for salty, deep-fried food hits, this is the place. Burgers, fries, onion rings, shakes, soda—the usual cardiac arrest suspects. Tacos and some other Mexican items are available, too. Lunch and dinner. ($)

BULLDOG CAFÉ

(1680 Mission Drive ☎ 805.686.9770
🖱 bookloftsolvang.com/bulldogcafe.htm) The Bulldog Café serves as a meeting place for locals, a rest stop for cyclists, and a navigation landmark with its life-size bulldog and water dish sculpture in front. (Yes, the water dish is filled for thirsty canines.) Architecturally part of **The Book Loft** and the **Hans Christian Andersen Museum**, the small café boasts a big menu of sandwiches, smoothies and baked goods, which are decidedly not Old World Danish. Chocolate zucchini muffins may sound a bit odd to the visitor, but to repeat customers they are heaven. The Bulldog is a friendly, busy place, and maybe the line would move more quickly if there weren't so much chitchat, but conversation and social niceties are slices of Solvang you can't bake in an oven. ($)

COWBOY WAY BBQ

(485 Alisal Rd. ☎ 805.691.9194) Head 'em up, move 'em out! There's a new restaurant in town and it is all about the meat. Located on the second floor of King Frederik's Court (down the street from the inn of the same name) the Cowboy Way BBQ is roomy, casual, and comfortable. The slowly cooked meats include tri-tip, pulled pork, and brisket, to name a few. Macaroni and cheese, potato salad, baked beans, and cornbread are the reliable side dishes. Open for lunch and dinner. Closed Tuesday. ($$)

EURO PANINI

(485 Alisal Rd. ☎ 805.688.0202) Don't let the name fool you, there is a lot of American in this little shop – like the Chinese chicken salad. The panini sandwiches are made on focaccia bread with options like chicken breast, pesto, and different cheeses. Euro Panini, which shares space with the frozen yogurt purveyor Whip a Peel, is perfect for a quick pick-me-up. ($)

PANINO

(475 First St. ☎ 805.688.0608 🖱 paninorestaurants.com) Panino serves up soups, salads, and sandwiches with Mediterranean zest. Prosciutto, salami, mozzarella, roasted red peppers, basil, and sun-dried tomatoes are frequently used ingredients. Add in the beer on tap and a large patio, and that equals a busy restaurant. Lunch only. ($)

RIVER GRILL AT THE ALISAL

(150 Alisal Rd. ☎ 805.688.7784) The beautiful golf course setting is worth the two-minute car ride or the 15-minute walk.

The faux rustic interior gives the restaurant a cabin or mountain lodge atmosphere. Breakfasts are standard American fare and the portions are hearty—it is burgers, hot and cold sandwiches, salads, soups, and a pasta choice for lunch. The dinner menu has a "home style" section, which includes entrees such as meatloaf, seared pork chops, and bacon-wrapped filet mignon. There are seafood specials most nights. ($$)

SOLVANG BREWING COMPANY

(1547 Mission Dr. ☎ 805.688.2337 🖰 solvangbrew.com) Just untapped in the Danish Capital of America, the Solvang Brewing Company is an oasis of beer in the valley of grapes. The beer is brewed on site (the former Danish Inn) and the rotating menu includes a hefeweizen, stout, pale ale, and seasonal drafts. There is a full bar, too. Many of the restaurant's recipes have beer as an ingredient. The fare is pub grub—burgers, hot sandwiches, and salads—with Solvang-Danish touches such as medisterpolse (Danish sausage) and Mexican spice (jalapeño sausage). Look for the big windmill in the middle of Mission Drive in the Village, that's the Solvang Brewing Company. ($$)

THE WILLOWS

(Chumash Casino Resort, 3400 E. Hwy 246, Santa Ynez ☎ 800.248.6274 🖰 chumashcasino.com) Upscale and up market with a sophisticated décor, The Willows specializes in steaks and seafood. The elegant atmosphere extends to the outdoor patio and private rooms. Entrees include surf and turf options, rack of lamb chops, different steak cuts, lobster tail, cioppino, chicken piccata, linguini and scampi, seared ahi tuna and more. The Willows has a *AAA Four Diamond* rating, and is the only restaurant at a tribal casino to earn the distinction. Cocktails and an extensive choice of local and imported wines. Open daily from 5 p.m. Reservations are recommended. ($$$)

TOWER PIZZA – FAMILY SPORTS DUGOUT

(436 Alisal Rd., Suites C&D ☎ 805.688.3036) This family-friendly, sports-centric pizza palace is in the courtyard behind the windmill on Alisal Road. Patio seating is available but the view to one of the eight televisions may be compromised. Children are welcome and there are video games for them. It's a noisy, fun establishment. In addition to pizza, sandwiches, salads, and pasta highlight the menu. Pets are allowed on the patio. The reason it is called Tower Pizza is because it sits in the shadow of the **Rundetårn** (Round Tower) replica. ($/$$)

WINE COUNTRY CUISINE

There isn't a strict definition to wine country cuisine. The concept, as old as agriculture itself, is farm-to-table freshness. Produce is a star ingredient in the cooking. Their flavors are allowed to speak for themselves rather than being drowned by sauces. Typically, meats and dairy products are organic and from small farms. Given the role of Italian immigrants in the history of California winemaking, Mediterranean flavors influence the tastes and seasonings of wine country cooking. The cuisine is not about cooking with wine, but diners can expect suggested wine pairings for menu items. Wine country cuisine is heartier and portions more generous than that of its California cuisine cousin.

CAFÉ ANGELICA

(490 First St. ☎ 805.686.9770) Café Angelica is frequently recommended by locals as the place for great food at a reasonable price. The friendly restaurant sits across from **Solvang Park**. The candlelight gives an air of romance to the dining room. The covered patio keeps things cool in the summer. Sample menu items are stuffed filet mignon, chicken Marsala, and filet mignon linguini Bolognese. There is a nice selection of local wines, and the dessert menu deserves saving room for. Lunch and dinner. ($$/$$$)

FRESCO VALLEY CAFÉ

(448 Atterdag Ave. ☎ 805.688.8857) Sitting at the foot of Atterdag Avenue and new to the Solvang restaurant scene, Fresco Valley Café is an outpost to a popular Santa Barbara eatery. The brick patio and fountain make a pretty outdoor setting, and the fireplace adds to the warmth of the interior. The salad, sandwiches, burgers, pizza, and wraps menu is deceptively casual. The cooking is a labor of love and made with the amore of Mediterranean ingredients and passion. Before deciding on entrees, take a look at the homemade desserts. An ordering strategy may be required. Wine and beer are available. Serving lunch and dinner. ($$)

HADSTEN HOUSE RESTAURANT

(1450 Mission Dr. ☎ 805.688.3210 🖱 hadstenhouse.com) Located at the Hadsten House Inn, the restaurant is open for dinner only. The ambience is contemporary, upscale, and romantic. The rotating menu always features vegetarian options, and its updates on classic comfort foods are very popular. Think a new take on fries, pork chops, steaks, and the like. The wine list pays homage to local vineyards. Beer and wine are the only alcohol served. Children's menu is available. Open daily. ($$$)

MIRABELLE RESTAURANT

(409 First St. ☎ 805.688.1703 🍷 solvanginns.com) Take the atmosphere of European elegance created by master restaurateurs Brigitte Guehr and Norbert Schultz. Wrap it around an award-winning wine list (*Wine Spectator* Award of Excellence 2010). Add innovative wine country cuisine by a master chef. Now you have the recipe for Mirabelle's success. There is extra seasoning such as a weekly rotating menu, a rare selection of older Napa, Sonoma, and French vintages, and professional attentive service. Past main course dishes include grilled filet steak with potato cheddar fondue, diver sea scallops sauteed in smoked paprika butter with Dungeness crabmeat risotto, and a vegetarian trio: goat cheese relleno, risotto timbal, and coconut soup. Available for private parties and events. Sadly, the Mirabelle is only open for dinner Thursday through Sunday, from 5 p.m. Reservations are recommended; the dining room seats only 26 guests. ($$/$$$)

ROOT 246 ✪ Must See!

(420 Alisal Rd. ☎ 805.686.8681 🍷 root-246.com) Foodies from around the globe make pilgrimages to Root 246, a restaurant by Bradley Ogden and owned by the Santa Ynez Band of Chumash Indians. There are reports of tears and near hysteria upon espying the celebrity Chef Ogden, the brains behind Solvang's first spot on the culinary map. He is a James Beard Award winner and his impressive resume includes restaurants in San Francisco and Las Vegas. Changing daily, the menu is based on the farm-to-table concept, putting the priority on freshness, simplicity, and sustainable agriculture. A prix fixe choice is always included in the menu.

Root 246 is next door to Hotel Corque and they share an upscale vibe and contemporary design. In addition to the booth and table seating in the main dining room, there are banquet facilities and a table in the kitchen for the fanatical foodie devotees. The kitchen table can be just for fun and something different, too. The full liquor license keeps the cocktails flowing in the two lounges. A "wall of wine," where about 1,800 bottles are kept, is a decorating statement. Live music on the patio follows a random schedule, and the open fountain court area is perfect for a standing cocktail party.

Given the caliber of food and service along with the famous label attached to it, Root 246, the prices at Root 246 are not out of line. Open for dinner only. ($$/$$$)

A LITTLE ETHNIC FLAIR

Even the most international of palates can satisfy their cravings in Solvang. Asian delights such as sushi are readily available. There is plenty of spicy Mexican to heat things up. Characterized by beans, rice, tortillas (flat bread made from corn or flour), salsa and/or peppers, Mexican food hardly qualifies as "international" in Southern California; the cuisine varies by region, though, and some of them are served in Solvang. Remember, the smaller the pepper the hotter it is.

KABUKI

(Japanese, 443 Second St. ☎ 805.693.0437) Across the street from **Solvang Theaterfest** is an intimate, small sushi bar with bright, blonde wood, white walls, and folk art touches that decorate the walls and tabletops. Concessions have been made for the American palate's love for novelty rolls filled with fried bits. The sushi master makes each dish upon ordering, as sushi should be done. Lunch is sushi only. The dinner menu offers sushi plus traditional Japanese fare such as teriyaki and donburi. There is a tasting menu, a chef's choice thing. The 5 to 6:30 p.m. happy hour menu has reduced prices on appetizers. Combination plates are offered at dinner. Good food. Closed on Mondays. ($$)

THE MANDARIN TOUCH

(Chinese, 1635 Mission Dr. ☎ 805.686.0222) American-familiar dishes such as chicken chow mein, fried wontons, and pork fried rice are the basics of the menu. There are more daring dishes, too, such as tofu with black mushrooms. Fortune cookies come with the check. There is a full bar. The restaurant's modern in look—no dragons on the wall or pagoda-like lanterns. For basic Chinese food, The Mandarin Touch is a little expensive. ($$)

MANNY'S

(Mexican, 1693 Mission Dr. ☎ 805.691.9137) The original Manny's closed more than a few years ago, much to the dismay of the townsfolk. Now they are smiling again because the second generation brought the family-run eatery back to life, and features regional Mexican cuisine. The Durango-style Mexican food...fajitas, tamales, chicken en mole, camarones rancheros. There's an evolving menu with new dishes weekly. The breakfast menu is a cross-cultural affair including, for example, Mexican huevos rancheros, American biscuits and gravy, Danish sausage pancakes, and a whole lot more. Large dining area for groups and parties. Open for breakfast, lunch, and dinner. Closed Tuesdays. ($/$$)

TACO ROCO

(Mexican, 614 Alamo Pintado Rd. ☎ 805.686.1901 ● tacoroco.com) About a half-mile out of the Village in Nielsen's Shopping Center, Taco Roco serves breakfast, lunch, and dinner. It has the look of an unassuming strip mall restaurant, but packs a powerful punch with cooked-to-order and made-with-love food. The unpretentious interior has comfy booths, self-serve fountain drinks, salsa bar, and walk-up order counter. As the name suggests, tacos are a specialty and come in both the soft and crispy varieties. Burritos, quesadillas, chile rellenos, and other Mexican favorites round out the menu. There are daily specials, and menudo is a Sunday favorite. Open daily. ($)

CREEKSIDE BUFFET

(Chumash Casino Resort, 3400 E. Highway 246, Santa Ynez ☎ 800.248.6274 ● chumashcasino.com) Most likely, the majority of hungry diners in the long line are locals. Who better to know a good thing? For all you can eat, the price can't be beat. However, the lines are long because the food is *so* good. The buffet has theme nights: Fiesta Mexicana, Sushi, and Seafood Celebrations, for example. Regional dishes, made-to-order entree stations, matching ethnic music, and a party atmosphere come with the flat fee price, as can lobster, king crab legs, prime rib, sashimi, and more. Here's how to do it like an insider: come early, stuff yourself, go back for more, and then more, leave late. Open daily for lunch and dinner. The lunch buffet is low key, but still oh so good. The blow-out dinner buffet begins mid to late afternoon. Check via the Internet or phone for special theme nights—it's worth it. ($$)

SNACKS AND SUCH

Dining

The aebleskiver haven't completely digested, but there's room for a little something more. Not a meal, just a couple of bites. Savory or sweet, there are plenty of snacks in Solvang.

OLD DANISH FOOD FARM, INC.

(441 Alisal Rd. ☎ 805.688.9932 🖱 solvangfudge.com) They farm fudge here. They do it the Mackinac Island way, by hand using copper kettles, marble slabs, fresh cream, and butter. In the mood for something not so sweet? There are soft pretzels with cheese. Old Danish Food Farm specializes mostly in sweets—caramel apples, peanut brittle, and, of course, Danish butter cookies. Old Danish Food Farm has been in business since 1961.

INGEBORG'S

(1679 Copenhagen Dr. ☎ 805.688.5612 🖱 ingeborgs.com) It's a toss-up whether the handmade Danish chocolates or the ice cream counter bring in the crowds. No matter, though, because visitors usually end up buying goodies from both sides of the shop. The chocolate here really is of the gourmet variety. Every day, candy-makers pack boxes of truffles, nut clusters, patties, orange and raspberry sticks—and that's just for starters.

Two of Ingeborg's specialties are a marzipan nougat log and a cornucopia made of chocolate filled with other chocolate pieces. Don't forget to check out the back of the candy store, too. There's a good selection of imported licorice and hard candies. ($)

RHYTHMS

(1694-B Copenhagen Dr. ☎ 805.686.5678) Zip in, zip out. That's the beat at Rhythms, which specializes in hot and ice-blended coffee drinks. Sometimes, only coffee—good coffee!—will do. Other little bits and bites are served, as well as 100 percent fruit smoothies. ($)

WHIP A PEEL

(485 Alisal Rd. ☎ 805.688.0202) Frozen yogurt is the perfect antidote to Solvang's sizzling hot summers. This wee little shop has tart and vanilla frozen yogurt. Their fresh fruit toppings are cut daily. Fruit smoothies are offered, too. ($)

PICNICS AND PARTIES

With all the surrounding vineyards and countryside it would be a shame not to have a picnic lunch or outdoor party. Pack a hodgepodge of goodies and spend time discussing where to eat dinner.

EL RANCHO MARKET ✪ Must See!

(2886 Mission Dr. ☎ 805.688.4300 ☺ elranchomarket.com) Man, this place is great. It is huge, clean, and chockablock full of high-end groceries with plenty of ready-to-eat options, including a full-service deli and gourmet sandwiches. For the requisite nosh while wine tasting, there is a section of artisanal cheese and fresh baked breads. Or, forget the wine tasting rooms and beeline for the extensive wine collection. Give serious consideration to using the hotel barbecue or firing up one in a park, this meat section can't be beat. Shoppers come from miles around to get their beef here. Their house-made chili gets rave reviews. Stock up on some specialty items to bring home. Live music on the weekends for the shoppers' entertainment.

NEW FRONTIERS NATURAL MARKETPLACE

(1984 Old Mission Dr. ☎ 805.693.1746) There's a friendly, busy atmosphere in this health-conscious grocery store. In addition to the standard organic packaged goods, the deli case offers fabulous salads and made-to-order sandwiches. There are baked goods specialties, too. At lunch time, the line is long—a good indication of a good place.

NIELSEN'S MARKET

(608 Alamo Pintado Rd. ☎ 805.688.3236

🌐 nielsensmarket.com) Nielsen's Market was the first supermarket in the Santa Ynez Valley. Danish sausage and other Scandinavian groceries such as tinned fish, cheeses, and cookies share shelf space with items typically found in American supermarkets. Perhaps needless to say, the wine selection is vast and there is a large stock of liquor and beer. The full bakery and meat counter, including fish, are popular with the locals. The deli section has party trays, sandwiches, and other to-go meals. Though it has been around since 1911, Nielsen's has kept up with changes in the marketplace—and specialty food items can be ordered through their website.

SOLVANG MARKET

(475 Fifth St. ☎ 805.686.5708) Open until 11 p.m., the Solvang Market can be a lifesaver in early to bed, early to rise Solvang. The inventory is generic, which is what's needed when looking for a toothbrush or some sunscreen. Keep Solvang Market in the back of your mind. The snack foods, selection of wine and beer, and ATM may come in handy one late night.

VIN HUS

(440 Alisal Rd. ☎ 805.686.5708 ☗ solvangvinhus.com) Stock up on imported food items for a picnic or for home. The international cheese and meat collections are impressive. Jams, jellies, and other sweets are well represented, too. Pickled beets and pickled cucumbers are nostalgic favorite tastes from Denmark. At most establishments in the Santa Ynez Valley, beer is hardly given any shelf space in comparison to wine, but not at Vin Hus. There's a wide assortment available. (Wine tasting is available here, too.) Shop here hungry, leave here broke.

Daytrips Near Solvang

⭐

Solvang is a great town and also has a lot of wonderful towns, attractions, and activities around it. The Danish pioneers certainly left their imprint on the local culture and so did the cowboys who came before them. The cowboy spirit is alive and well in the Santa Ynez Valley. You probably already guessed that by the number of cowboy hats and boots you've seen. The grapevine spreads beyond Solvang, too. It reaches north into the Santa Maria trail and east into the Lompoc wine ghetto. Some real fun is riding its twisting and winding branches on the *Sideways* trail.

GETTING OUT OF DODGE

A short 15- to 20-minute drive from Solvang finds horseback riding stables, or a lake to go boating or fishing. The countryside scenery is lovely, and it's always exciting to see wild animals.

CACHUMA LAKE RECREATION AREA

(2225 Highway 154, Santa Ynez Valley ☎ 805.686.5050/weekdays ☎ 805.686.5055/weekends ☗ cachuma.com) While there's lots to do at the Cachuma Lake Recreation Area, swimming in the lake isn't one of them. However, two pools are open from Memorial Day through Labor Day. Swimming isn't permitted in the lake because Cachuma is a domestic water supply, so water-skiing, canoes, kayaks, windsurfing, or any other body contact with the water is also prohibited.

Don't worry—you'll find plenty to do. For fishing, there are boat rentals, boat launch, marina, fishing equipment, and licenses available. Other activities include day-use picnic areas, basketball courts, playgrounds, and horseshoe pits. There is a general store in the compound, too. The area's **Nature Center** (805.693.0691) was founded in 1988, with a focus on educational activities, such as nature walks and hikes. The center's exhibits are hands on and geared toward children—there are often students on field trips. Visitors can feel animal fur in the Wild Animal Room and measure the wingspan of feathered friends in the Bird Room. A number local Chumash artifacts are on display at the center, including jewelry and bead money. Other than possible high winds, Cachuma Lake Recreation Area is a great place to spend the day. It can be very windy.

LA PURISIMA MISSION

(2295 Purisima Rd., Lompoc ☎ 805.773.3713

⬤ **lapurisimamission.org)** La Purisima Mission (or locally, La Purisima) is the only California example of a complete Spanish Catholic mission complex. It was founded in 1787 on December 8, the feast day of the Immaculate Conception. Self-guided tours are from 9 a.m. to 5 p.m. Meet at the Visitors Center at 1 p.m. for free guided tours, which last about 60 to 90 minutes. Ten of La Purisima's original buildings have been restored, as well as the aqueduct and water system. There is a five-acre garden and livestock, including burros, longhorn cattle, sheep, and goats. The mission is not used currently as a parish. La Purisima shares a similar history to Mission Santa Inés, in that the Spanish colonizers killed a lot of the native people. This explains, many believe, the many ghostly legends connected to La Purisima. Paranormal activity such as whispers and cold drafts are said to be spirits of Chumash who died at La Purisima. There is a vehicle admission charge, starting at

$6 for private vehicle through $100 for buses. There are picnic tables. Open daily.

NATURE CRUISES

(☎ 805.686.5050, or make reservation at main gate
⛊ countyofsb.org) The Cachuma Lake Nature Cruise is a two-hour boat ride narrated by a naturalist versed in local flora and fauna. Available year-round, the *Osprey*, a 30-passenger pontoon boat, explores Cachuma's rich plant and animal wildlife. The winter season affords sightings of resident and migratory bald eagles and waterfowl. In springtime, be sure to bring sunglasses for the show-stopping carpet of psychedelic-colored wildflowers. Nest-building birds and does with fawns are two other stars of the springtime nature show. The cruise is best suited for nature lovers age four and older. The pontoon boat is wheelchair accessible. Winter Eagle Cruises are November through February, and Summer Wildlife Cruises are March through October. Reservations are required. Tickets are from $7 for children.

SANTA YNEZ VALLEY HISTORICAL MUSEUM AND PARKS – JANEWAY CARRIAGE HOUSE

(3596 Sagunto St., Santa Ynez ☎ 805.688.7889
⛊ santaynezmusuem.org) This museum houses a collection and exhibit of the area's history from its earliest inhabitants, the Chumash, through its ranching heritage to the founding of the valley's five towns. With its model train diorama of the Pacific Coast Railway and collection of American carriages, saddles, and tack, this place is of particular interest to the Old West enthusiast. ($)

SADDLE UP

Horses and everything equestrian is popular in the Santa Ynez Valley. There are horseback riding stables and equestrian events scattered around the valley. Beginners as well as accomplished riders are equally at home in the stables around here.

RANCHO OSO GUEST RANCH & STABLES

(3750 Paradise Rd., Santa Barbara ☎ 805.683.5110 📱 rancho-oso.com) A public riding stable that offers different-length trail rides for beginners and more experienced riders. Rides are open to children age eight and up. Safety equipment is provided. Rancho Oso is located about 30 minutes from Solvang. ($/$$)

VINO VAQUEROS

(☎ 805.944.0493 📱 vinovaqueros.com) The private rides have a wine country focus. There are tasting rides, lunch rides, and more. Beginners are welcome. ($$$)

GETTING SOME GRUB

There are excellent eating options in the Santa Ynez Valley. A number of establishments have remained true to their Old West heritage. Others have started making history on their own.

ANDERSEN'S PEA SOUP

(376 Avenue of the Flags, Buellton ☎ 805.688.5581 📱 peasoupandersens.net) This roadside restaurant is famous up and down the coast of California. Many a family vacation has included a pea soup stop, a tradition that still continues today. The easy-off-and-on freeway access can't be beat and the parking lot is roomy. The gift shop is pretty nifty, too. For really good food, check out many of the other nearby eateries. ($$)

BROTHERS RESTAURANT AT MATTEI'S TAVERN

(2350 Railroad Ave., Los Olivos ☎ 805.688.8965 🖰 matteistavern.com) Still in its original building, Mattei's Tavern dates back to 1886 when it was a stagecoach stop. Today it is fine dining with the best steaks, fresh seafood, and organic produce. The romantic setting harkens back to an earlier era with vintage photos and multiple fireplaces. Local wines and imports make up the wine list. ($$/$$$)

COLD SPRING TAVERN

(5995 Stagecoach Rd., Santa Barbara ☎ 805.967.0066 🖰 coldspringtavern.com) The address reads Santa Barbara, but the tavern is on the Santa Ynez Valley side of the mountains. Built in the 1860s as a stagecoach stop, Cold Spring Tavern continues to do a brisk business with hearty meals in a romantic setting. The structure's rock fireplace and wooden walls keep the Old West feel alive, as does the venison entree on the menu. Live music on the weekends brings in the crowds from the Santa Barbara side of the mountains. The tavern also serves as a pit stop for lots of motorcycle clubs. Pay attention to the name of the place—it is cold inside! Breakfast is served on Saturday and Sunday only. Lunch and dinner served daily. Dinner reservations are requested. ($$/$$$)

ELLEN'S PANCAKE HOUSE

(272 Avenue of the Flags, Buellton ☎ 805.688.5312) Start a day of wine tasting here. Put down one of these hearty breakfasts and you won't be hungry until past dinnertime. There's lot more here than just pancakes—omelets, chicken fried steak, pork chops, salad, and other diner favorites. Breakfast, lunch, and dinner. On Mondays, breakfast and lunch only. ($/$$)

THE BALLARD INN RESTAURANT ✪ Must See!

(2436 Baseline Ave., Ballard ☎ 805.688.7770

🖰 **ballardinn.com)** A favorite among locals, visitors, restaurant critics, and a variety of judges who give out awards, The Ballard Inn's menu features east-meets-west fusion fare. For example, one appetizer is "new style hamachi sashimi with avocado and soy-yuzu vinaigrette," and an entree is pan-seared duck breast with sweet potato puree and balsamic reduction. The setting is impossibly romantic in a cozy dining room with a fireplace and candlelight. Dinner only. Open to the public Wednesday through Sunday. Guests of the inn have first dibs on dining in the restaurant. Call for a reservation. ($$$)

TRATTORIA GRAPPOLO

(3687 Sagunto St., Santa Ynez ☎ 805.688.6899

🖰 **trattoriagrappolo.com)** Now that's Italian! Grappolo serves up risotto, tortellini, cioppino, pizza, and other favorites in a convivial atmosphere. The menu is a natural complement to a day of wine tasting. It's a locals' favorite. Ask about the available cooking classes. ($$)

AS SEEN IN *SIDEWAYS*

The wineries featured in *Sideways* weren't just chosen for their beautiful scenery—they do make great wine! Take a taste of where some of the most memorable scenes were filmed. All are open daily. Of course, it wasn't all vineyards and wine in *Sideways*. The characters did eat and explore other parts of the area, too.. Double-check hours for all establishments listed here.

AJ SPURS

(350 E. Hwy 246, Buellton ☎ 805.686.1655 🖱 ajspurs.com) Hearty Old West–style dining with lots of barbecued meats in the menu. The beans are a favorite. In the movie, Jack gets tangled up with Cami, a waitress at this restaurant. Dinner only. ($$)

BUELLTON WINDMILL DAYS INN

(114 E. Hwy 246, Buellton ☎ 805.688.8448) This is where Miles and Jack stayed in the movie *Sideways* and where Stephanie beat up Jack. Other than the being able to say "I stayed at the motel with the big windmill," there's no compelling reason to bunk here. There's a local hangout bar/sports lounge with a large television on the premises. There are 108 guest rooms, guest laundry, an outdoor swimming pool, and Jacuzzi. Complimentary continental breakfast is served. ($$)

FESS PARKER WINERY

(6200 Foxen Canyon Rd., Los Olivos ☎ 805.688.8554 🖱 fessparker.com) Yep, it's the same Fess Parker of Daniel Boone fame. Called Frass Canyon in the movie, this is where the unforgettable scene of Miles downing the spit bucket was filmed. Fess Parker Winery is a beautiful spot.

FOXEN WINERY

(7200 Foxen Canyon Rd.. Santa Maria ☎ 805.937.4251
🖱 **foxenvineyard.com)** There's a new solar-powered tasting room here, but don't worry, the "shack" featured in *Sideways* is still in operation. This is the winery where Miles and Jack sneak wine when the pourer's back is turned.

HITCHING POST II

(406 E. Highway 246, Buellton ☎ 805.688.0676
🖱 **hitchingpost2.com)** The Hitching Post II is about the oak barbecue, and beef rules the menu. The Hitching Post also produces its own label of wine, and it's a good one, too. In *Sideways*, Miles and Jack eat dinner here and talk with Maya, a waitress. ($$)

KALYRA WINERY

(3 N. Refugio Rd., Santa Ynez ☎ 805.693.8864
🖱 **kalyrawinery.com)** *Sideways* fame seems to have gone to the tasting room's head. It is expensive, filled with "official" souvenirs, and there's a singles scene vibe, which can be fun if that's the plan for the day. At any rate, the wine is good. This is the winery where Jack and Miles meet Stephanie, who works at the winery.

LOS OLIVOS CAFÉ & WINE MERCHANT

(2879 Grand Ave., Los Olivos ☎ 888.946.3748
🖱 **losolivoscafe.com)** The seasonal menu is made from local, organic, and sustainable ingredients. It's a popular place with

plenty of good reasons why—starting with the food. The *Sideways* characters eat dinner here and share several bottles of wine. Lunch and dinner. ($$)

OSTRICHLAND USA

(610 E. Highway 246, Buellton ☎ 805.686.9696

💧 **ostrichlandusa.com)** You can't miss this place unless, of course, the birds have their heads in the ground. Emus are as much a part of the landscape as the ostriches are. This is a 33-acre breeding farm and the public is invited to view the flightless birds—from either up close or far away. The birds here are not sold for meat, but you can buy their eggs either fresh or as decorative items. Open daily, including holidays, from 10 a.m. to sunset.

THE LOMPOC WINE GHETTO TRAIL

Lompoc (say *lom-poke*, not *lom-pock*) is known primarily for its federal prison and Vandenberg Air Force Base. In certain circles, though, it is famous as the "Gateway to the Santa Rita Hills Wine Country." Santa Rita Hills is one of Santa Barbara County's wine appellations. To reach the "ghetto" from Solvang, go west on Highway 246/Mission Drive past vineyards and flower fields (flower seeds are big business in Lompoc) for 15 miles or so. There will be a stoplight; this is the intersection of Twelfth and Industrial Way. Look for the "Sobhani Industrial Park" sign. Don't expect the usual wine country Mediterranean-inspired tasting rooms. These 20 or so wineries are too busy perfecting their craft to get bogged down with that sort of thing. Here it is all about the wine, and only the wine. Tasting in the ghetto is a weekend thing or by appointment. Scout around. There are a lot of rising stars in the ghetto. Better hurry, the nearby billboard reads "Santa Rita Hills Wine Center Coming Soon."

FIDDLEHEAD

**(1597 E. Chestnut Ave., Lompoc ☎ 800.251.1225
📱 fiddleheadcellars.com)** Miles calls the sauvignon blanc "terrific" in *Sideways*. The pinot noir has a loyal following, too. Both are sustainably produced. Open Friday and Saturday from 11 a.m. to 4 p.m., or by appointment.

FLYING GOAT CELLARS

**(1520 E. Chestnut Ct., Unit A, Lompoc ☎ 805.736.9032
📱 flyinggoatcellars.com)** This is particularly for the pinot noir lover. Handcrafted. Thursday through Saturday 11 a.m. to 4 p.m., or by appointment.

SAMSARA

**(1500 E. Chestnut Ct., Unit A, Lompoc ☎ 805.331.2292
📱 samsarawine.com)** The Samsara vintners employ a hands-off style to make their pinot noir and Syrah. Open Friday through Sunday noon to 4 p.m., or by appointment.

THE SANTA MARIA WINE TRAIL

The Santa Maria Wine Trail in north Santa Barbara County covers a big area. Wineries are spread out and the landscape alternates between vineyards and other fields. A full tank of gas and full stomach are a good idea before starting out. There are some snack options at the wineries. Being further afield, the scene is a bit quieter, but it does reach raucous levels on weekend afternoons. These wineries, listed alphabetically, are open daily. The **Santa Maria Valley Chamber of Commerce and Visitor & Convention Bureau** (☎ *800.331.3779* 🖱 *santamaria. com)* has plenty more information on the Santa Maria Wine Trail. So does the **Santa Barbara County Vintners Association** (☎ *805.688.0881* 🖱 *sbcountywines.com).*

COTTONWOOD CANYON VINEYARD & WINERY

(3940 Dominion Rd., Santa Maria ☎ 805.937.8463
🖱 **cottonwoodcanyon.com)** The Cottonwood tasting room is in the middle of the wine-making action. It's the kind of place that expects dirt from the fields to be tracked inside. On Saturdays there are special tours of the wine caves. Chardonnay, pinot noir, and Syrah are the favorite pours at this friendly place.

KENNETH VOLK VINEYARDS

(5230 Tepusquet Rd., Santa Maria ☎ 805.938.7896
🖱 **volkwines.com)** The Kenneth Volk Vineyards specializes in pinot noir and chardonnay. The wood-paneled tasting room is cozy, and the sociable staff shares restaurant recommendations and other opinions on how to spend a day on the Santa Maria Trail. In front of the tasting room are a few tables with umbrellas; in the back is a lanai with more seating.

RANCHO SISQUOC WINERY

(6600 Foxen Canyon Rd., Santa Maria ☎ 805.934.4332
🖱 **ranchosisquoc.com)** To say the driveway to Rancho Sisquoc is long is an understatement, so don't think you missed a turn somewhere. The tasting room exterior looks kind of like a wine barrel and falls almost into the category of cute. There is a large park-like outside seating area perfect for picnics. One of

Santa Barbara County's first wineries, Rancho Sisquoc grows Bordeaux, Burgundy, and Tuscan varietals. The price of a tasting includes the really pretty etched-glass tasting glass.

RIVERBENCH VINEYARD & WINERY
(6020 Foxen Canyon Rd., Santa Maria ☎ 805.937.8340)
Specializing in chardonnay and pinot noir, Riverbench has been growing grapes since 1973. With their 2006 harvest, they began making wine. The tasting room is in a gorgeously restored craftsman-style home, which is worth a look, even if you're not wine tasting. Enjoy the view from the outdoor patio. Make an appointment for a winery tour.

EATING IN THE SANTA MARIA AREA

There's more to eating in Santa Maria than their famous Santa Maria Style Barbecue, though that is reason enough to eat here. Santa Maria style uses tri-tip and top-block sirloin. Seasoned with garlic salt and pepper, the meat is cooked over red oak. Pinquinto beans are the traditional side dish. Santa Maria Style Barbecue originated during California's El Rancho period.

CHEF RICK'S
(4869 South Bradley Rd., Santa Maria ☎ 805.937.9512
⬤ chefricks.com) Another case of don't judge a restaurant by its strip mall location. The food is a fusion of cuisines with a foundation of New Orleans cooking—for example, crispy catfish with pickled jalapeño tartar sauce. Check out the daily specials. It's Chef Rick himself in the kitchen, with help of course, pumping out the food, so sometimes the food takes longer than one expects it to reach the table. Made with love, it

is well worth the wait. The emphasis is on fun for the atmosphere and décor—loud, bright, purple, cordial, and tons of good food plus a killer wine list. Think "big picture" when ordering because you want to be able to have dessert. Lunch and dinner. ($$)

SANTA MARIA INN'S GARDEN ROOM

(801 South Broadway, Santa Maria ☎ 805.346.7908 ⏚ santamariainn.com) "Historic" is an official part of the inn's name, and its beautiful buildings and landscaping are certainly heirloom quality. The Garden Room offers breakfast, lunch, dinner, and brunch on Sunday. The brunch is spectacular with tables laden with salads, side dishes, entrees, and desserts (several tables with different desserts). There is a carving station, an omelet bar, and endless choices. The dinner menu is impressive, too. Pastas, fresh seafood, and beef entrees come with hearty sides. Santa Maria Barbecue Style tri-tip is a house favorite. The everyday breakfast offers a buffet, albeit a more modest affair than the one offered on Sunday, and ala carte items. The **Olde English Tap Room** and the Wine Cellar & Martini Bar are separate venues serving drinks. The Olde **English Tap Room** is the quieter of the two and has a selection of imported beers. The Wine Cellar & Martini Bar offers up signature martinis and a mega selection of Central Coast wines. ($$)

TRATTORIA ULIVETO

(285 S. Broadway, Orcutt ☎ 805.934.4546 ⏚ trattoriauliveto.com) Billed as traditional Italian cuisine, Trattoria Uliveto delivers American favorites prepared the way they should be. The menu is divided into antipasti, insalata, pizza, pasta, and dolci. Each of the Italian dishes comes with an English description; for example, Lombata di Maiale is breaded pork chops, arugula, tomato, and lemon. The extensive wine list features local, northern California, and Italian bottles. Desserts are worth saving room for. This is a pretty restaurant with a cozy atmosphere and Italian music playing. (Orcutt is the small bedroom community bordering Santa Maria.) Lunch and dinner. ($$)

Index

Index

Index

About the Author

Native Californian Amy Marie Orozco is a feature writer and journalist covering the state's Central Coast. Her favorite subjects are the interwoven back stories of people and places making up the area's brightly colored tapestry. Nowadays, bakeries and wine run neck and neck for Amy's number one reason for a drive to Solvang. An intrepid world traveler, wanderlust takes her to the far reaches of the globe, but she is always happy to return home to Santa Barbara County. She and her husband, Alonzo, make their home near the sea.

The cowboy spirit is alive and well in the Santa Ynez Valley. You probably already guessed that by the number of cowboy hats and boots you've seen.

ᐸ☆tourist
town guides®

Explore America's Fun Places

Books in the *Tourist Town Guides*® series are available at book-stores and online. You can also visit our website for additional book and travel information. The address is:

http://www.touristtown.com

Astoria

Astoria, Oregon was the West Coast's first permanent American settlement. The city and surrounding areas have been the location of choice for many Hollywood blockbusters as well as for vacationers looking to see the state's beautiful North Coast.

Price: $14.95; ISBN: 978-1-935455-08-0

Biloxi

Explore Biloxi and the Mississippi Gulf Coast. Find the best place to get a bowl of seafood gumbo and the most enjoyable golf course. From casinos to beaches, Biloxi and Gulfport offer great vacation opportunities.

Price: $14.95; ISBN: 978-1-935455-09-7

Black Hills (2nd Edition)

Revised and updated, use this guide to discover the striking natural beauty, abundant wildlife, and many attractions that the Black Hills has to offer, from the iconic Mount Rushmore to the historic Mammoth Site.

Price: $14.95; ISBN: 978-1-935455-10-3

Branson

Explore Branson, Missouri and the Ozarks. This completely independent guide will help you plan the perfect vacation, with information about the best shows in town and other attractions in the Lakes Area. Learn why many call Branson "America's favorite hometown."

Price: $14.95; ISBN: 978-1-935455-11-0

Deadwood

This independent book will help you plan the perfect vacation to the historic town of Deadwood, in the heart of South Dakota's Black Hills. Stroll the streets where Wild Bill Hickok and Calamity Jane once lived.

Price: $13.95; ISBN: 978-1-935455-22-6

Door County

This independent guide will help you plan the perfect vacation to Wisconsin's thumb, including must-see attractions and the best outdoor activities. Hit the streets shopping, sit down for dinner overlooking the water, and discover the hidden natural beauty of Door County.

Price: $14.95; ISBN: 978-1-935455-12-7

Fredericksburg

Explore Fredericksburg's must-see attractions, find the best places for wine enthusiasts, and learn about the area's German heritage with this independent guide. Get the most out of your next visit to the Texas Hill Country.

Price: $14.95; ISBN: 978-1-935455-13-4

Key West (3rd Edition)

There is much to see and do in Key West, a vacation hotspot welcoming millions of visitors each year. In this guide, learn about area beaches, restaurants and bars, Duval Street attractions, hotels, and more. This book will help you plan your next vacation to the Conch Republic.

Price: $14.95; ISBN: 978-1-935455-14-1

Lake Placid

Look down a ski jump, hike the high peaks, and learn to dogsled. Explore the picturesque Village of Lake Placid, New York, and the surrounding Adirondacks. Also discover the best of nearby Lake George and Saranac Lake.

Price: $14.95; ISBN: 978-1-935455-15-8

Mackinac (2nd Edition)

Nestled between Michigan's Upper and Lower Peninsulas, Mackinac Island is a favorite tourist destination and a beautiful getaway spot. This guide will help you plan your vacation to Mackinac Island and Mackinaw City.

Price: $14.95; ISBN: 978-1-935455-16-5

Madison County

Explore the picturesque landscape and historic covered bridges of Madison County, Iowa. Whether planning to photograph the bridges, sample the local wine, or take take a step back in time, make your journey a memorable one.

Price: $13.95; ISBN: 978-1-935455-17-2

Mystic

This guide to the historic Connecticut seaport city of Mystic will help you plan the perfect vacation, with comprehensive information about the Mystic Seaport, the best places to shop, dine and sleep, and must-see attractions.

Price: $14.95; ISBN: 978-1-935455-18-9

Salem

This independent guidebook will help you plan the perfect vacation to Massachusetts' historic seaport and site of the Salem Witch Trials, with information about the best historic attractions, Halloween and Haunted Happenings, and more.

Price: $14.95; ISBN: 978-1-935455-19-6

Sleepy Hollow

Washington Irving immortalized Sleepy Hollow and Tarrytown in his classic tale. This independent guide will help you plan the perfect vacation, with comprehensive information about must-see Historic Hudson Valley estates, facts and fictions of Sleepy Hollow, and more.

Price: $13.95; ISBN: 978-1-935455-20-2

Solvang

Plan the perfect vacation to America's Danish Capital. Learn about must-see area landmarks and highlights of the Santa Ynez Valley. From aebleskiver to vineyards and windmills, use this guide to travel prepared.

Price: $13.95; ISBN: 978-1-935455-21-9

tourist town guides

www.touristtown.com

Also Available

TITLE	ISBN	PRICE
Atlantic City	978-1-935455-00-2	$14.95
Breckenridge	978-0-9767064-9-6	$14.95
Frankenmuth	978-0-9767064-8-9	$13.95
Gatlinburg	978-1-935455-04-2	$14.95
Hershey	978-0-9792043-8-8	$13.95
Hilton Head	978-1-935455-06-6	$14.95
Jackson Hole	978-0-9792043-3-3	$14.95
Las Vegas	978-0-9792043-5-7	$14.95
Myrtle Beach	978-1-935455-01-1	$14.95
Niagara Falls	978-1-935455-03-5	$14.95
Ocean City	978-0-9767064-6-5	$13.95
Provincetown	978-1-935455-07-3	$13.95
Sandusky	978-0-9767064-5-8	$13.95
Williamsburg	978-1-935455-05-9	$14.95
Wisconsin Dells	978-0-9792043-9-5	$13.95

See http://www.touristtown.com for more information about any of these titles.

www.touristtown.com

ORDER FORM
ON REVERSE SIDE

Tourist Town Guides® is published by:
Channel Lake, Inc.
P.O. Box 1771
New York, NY 10156

ORDER FORM

Telephone: With your credit card handy,
call toll-free 800.592.1566

Fax: Send this form toll-free to 866.794.5507

E-mail: Send the information on this form
to orders@channellake.com

Postal mail: Send this form with payment to Channel Lake, Inc.
P.O. Box 1771, New York, NY, 10156

Your Information: ( ) Do not add me to your mailing list
Name: _____
Address: _____
City: _____ State: _____ Zip: _____
Telephone: _____
E-mail: _____

Book Title(s) / ISBN(s) / Quantity / Price
(see www.touristtown.com for this information)

_____

_____

_____

Total payment*: $_____
Payment Information: (Circle One) Visa / Mastercard
Number: _____ Exp: _____
Or, make check payable to: **Channel Lake, Inc.**

** Add the lesser of $6.50 USD or 18% of the total purchase price
for shipping. International orders call or e-mail first! New York
orders add 8% sales tax.*

www.touristtown.com

ORDER FORM
ON REVERSE SIDE

Tourist Town Guides® is published by:
Channel Lake, Inc.
P.O. Box 1771
New York, NY 10156

ORDER FORM

Telephone: With your credit card handy,
call toll-free 800.592.1566

Fax: Send this form toll-free to 866.794.5507

E-mail: Send the information on this form
to orders@channellake.com

Postal mail: Send this form with payment to Channel Lake, Inc.
P.O. Box 1771, New York, NY, 10156

Your Information: ( ) Do not add me to your mailing list

Name: _____

Address: _____

City: _____ State: _____ Zip: _____

Telephone: _____

E-mail: _____

Book Title(s) / ISBN(s) / Quantity / Price
(see www.touristtown.com for this information)

_____

_____

_____

Total payment*: $_____

Payment Information: (Circle One) Visa / Mastercard

Number: _____ Exp: _____

Or, make check payable to: **Channel Lake, Inc.**

* Add the lesser of $6.50 USD or 18% of the total purchase price for shipping. International orders call or e-mail first! New York orders add 8% sales tax.

www.touristtown.com

ORDER FORM
ON REVERSE SIDE

Tourist Town Guides® is published by:
Channel Lake, Inc.
P.O. Box 1771
New York, NY 10156

ORDER FORM

Telephone: With your credit card handy, call toll-free 800.592.1566

Fax: Send this form toll-free to 866.794.5507

E-mail: Send the information on this form to orders@channellake.com

Postal mail: Send this form with payment to Channel Lake, Inc. P.O. Box 1771, New York, NY, 10156

Your Information: ( ) Do not add me to your mailing list

Name: _____

Address: _____

City: _____ State: _____ Zip: _____

Telephone: _____

E-mail: _____

Book Title(s) / ISBN(s) / Quantity / Price
(see www.touristtown.com for this information)

_____

_____

_____

Total payment*: $_____

Payment Information: (Circle One)   Visa / Mastercard

Number: _____ Exp: _____

Or, make check payable to: **Channel Lake, Inc.**

* Add the lesser of $6.50 USD or 18% of the total purchase price for shipping. International orders call or e-mail first! New York orders add 8% sales tax.